Arduino Networking

Connect your projects to the Web using the Arduino
Ethernet library

Marco Schwartz

BIRMINGHAM - MUMBAI

Arduino Networking

First published: August 2014

Production reference: 1140814

Published by Packt Publishing Ltd.
Livery Place
35 Livery Street
Birmingham B3 2PB, UK.

ISBN 978-1-78398-686-6

www.packtpub.com

Cover image by Pratyush Mohanta (tysoncinematics@gmail.com)

Credits

Author
Marco Schwartz

Reviewers
C. M. Banas
Ryan Dunn
Phillip Mayhew
Tom O'Connor
Krisjanis Rijnieks

Commissioning Editor
Pramila Balan

Acquisition Editor
Harsha Bharwani

Content Development Editor
Sumeet Sawant

Technical Editors
Kunal Anil Gaikwad
Siddhi Rane

Copy Editors
Mradula Hegde
Adithi Shetty

Project Coordinator
Danuta Jones

Proofreader
Ameesha Green

Indexer
Rekha Nair

Production Coordinator
Melwyn D'sa

Cover Work
Melwyn D'sa

About the Author

Marco Schwartz is an electrical engineer, entrepreneur, and blogger. He has a Master's degree in Electrical Engineering and Computer Science from SUPELEC in France, and a Master's degree in Microengineering from EPFL in Switzerland.

He has more than 5 years of experience working in the domain of electrical engineering. His interests gravitate around electronics, home automation, the Arduino and the Raspberry Pi platforms, open source hardware projects, and 3D printing.

He runs several websites around Arduino, including the Open Home Automation website (http://www.openhomeautomation.net/), which is dedicated to building home automation systems using open source hardware.

He has written another book, *Home Automation with Arduino, Amazon Digital Services, Inc.*, which is a self-published Kindle book. He has also written a book on how to build Internet of Things projects with Arduino called *Internet of Things with the Arduino Yun, Packt Publishing*.

About the Reviewers

Ryan Dunn is a solutions architect, who specializes in web technologies and enterprise-level deployments. He currently lives in Southern Kansas City, KS.

He holds a Bachelor's degree in Computer Science from Kansas State University and a Master's degree in Business Administration from the University of Kansas. He has worked for a variety of organizations, with his career spanning a number of industries, including e-commerce, digital marketing, SEO, education, security, and mobile.

He has been working with web technologies for over 10 years, and during this time, he has always retained an agnostic approach to the technology, which has resulted in a wide range of experience. As a solutions architect, he manages every aspect of solution deployments, including analysis, network architecture, system architecture, creative design, and development.

> I have a wife, Crystal, and two children. As a result of their support, I have been able to pursue my passion for technology and am forever grateful for all their love.

Phillip Mayhew has a Bachelor of Science degree in Computer Science from North Carolina State University. He is the founder and managing principal of Rextency Technologies LLC, which is based in Statesville, North Carolina. His primary expertise lies in software application performance testing and monitoring.

Tom O'Connor is an experienced systems architect and DevOps engineer. He lives in the West Midlands in the United Kingdom. Over the last 8 years, he has worked for a wide variety of companies, from e-commerce to video effects, and now is the owner of the company he founded, which provides systems consultancy for wireless network design and installations.

He writes a technical blog on his website that provides both tutorial articles and updates on what he's been working on. He has wide-reaching skills and experience gathered over the last 10 years of working on Windows, Linux, and Unix systems for most of that time, coupled with recent experience in designing and building high-performance computer systems.

He is also an active member of the UK DevOps community as well as a community moderator on `www.serverfault.com`, where he demonstrates his expertise and skills to a wide audience.

Krisjanis Rijnieks is a digital interactive media professional working with projects that involve graphic design, animation, user interface design, projection mapping, programming, and electronics. The outcome of his projects usually are websites, games, and hardware prototypes or interactive installations. He also runs workshops in the field of creative coding and projection mapping. One of his most interesting current projects is the development of an openframeworks add-on for projection mapping on the Raspberry Pi—ofxPiMapper.

He is also an MA student at the Media Lab Helsinki (Aalto University School of Arts, Design and Architecture), and he is currently working on his master thesis, which is related to the ofxPiMapper projection mapping software project.

Krisjanis runs a small digital media company CodeBark (`www.codebark.com`) with his colleague, Irina Spicaka. Together, they also developed a platform called Creative Coding for Live Audio and Visuals (`www.cc4av.info`), which acts as a placeholder for different events and workshops related to electronic audiovisual culture.

He is also collaborating with the Fab Lab, Berlin, and this is where he spends most of his time when in Berlin.

Cinder – Begin Creative Coding, Packt Publishing, is the first book that he has worked on. It's an introduction to Cinder, the C++ creative coding framework, (similar to openFrameworks) and contains tutorials to get you started with Cinder as fast and painless as possible.

www.PacktPub.com

Support files, eBooks, discount offers, and more

You might want to visit www.PacktPub.com for support files and downloads related to your book.

Did you know that Packt offers eBook versions of every book published, with PDF and ePub files available? You can upgrade to the eBook version at www.PacktPub.com and as a print book customer, you are entitled to a discount on the eBook copy. Get in touch with us at service@packtpub.com for more details.

At www.PacktPub.com, you can also read a collection of free technical articles, sign up for a range of free newsletters and receive exclusive discounts and offers on Packt books and eBooks.

http://PacktLib.PacktPub.com

Do you need instant solutions to your IT questions? PacktLib is Packt's online digital book library. Here, you can access, read, and search across Packt's entire library of books.

Why subscribe?

- Fully searchable across every book published by Packt
- Copy and paste, print, and bookmark content
- On demand and accessible via web browser

Free access for Packt account holders

If you have an account with Packt at www.PacktPub.com, you can use this to access PacktLib today and view nine entirely free books. Simply use your login credentials for immediate access.

Table of Contents

Preface

Arduino is an amazing platform to quickly create exciting electronics projects. Using the Arduino platform, even non-experts can connect sensors, actuators, and displays together and build complex projects that provide immediate applications for everyday life.

However, these projects are even better when they are connected, meaning they have some way to communicate with other devices, and not necessarily with other Arduino boards. There are many ways to connect Arduino projects together and to other devices such as computers: WiFi, XBee, Bluetooth, and Ethernet. This book will focus entirely on how to create amazing projects using this latest technology to connect Arduino projects.

Using Ethernet has several advantages over wireless solutions: it is fast, cheap, and you will find plenty of help on the subject on the Internet. For me, the most important thing is that the Ethernet library for Arduino is very well documented, and comes built-in with the Arduino software. It's hardware counterpart, the Arduino Ethernet shield, is also very well built and well supported by the Arduino community.

In this book, we are going to see how to use the Ethernet shield and the Ethernet library via six exciting projects. We are going to start with the very basics and see how to connect the Ethernet shield to your local network and the Web. Then, we will send data from the Ethernet shield to a server located on your local network. Finally, we will integrate the Ethernet shield in an "Internet of Things" framework, by building several projects connected directly to the Web.

What this book covers

Chapter 1, *Discover the Arduino Ethernet Shield*, introduces the Arduino Ethernet shield by showing you how to set up everything so you can easily build more exciting applications in the next chapters. We are going to connect the Ethernet shield to your router, and make sure that it can access the Web.

Chapter 2, *Sending Data to a Web Server*, explains how to connect a temperature and humidity sensor to your Arduino board and use the Ethernet shield to send this data continuously to a web server running on your computer. We will also plot this data in real time on the web server so that you can visualize it in your browser.

Chapter 3, *Data Logging Station*, uses the same hardware as in the previous chapter, but we will make the Arduino Ethernet more independent. We will log the data measured by the board locally on an SD card, and also create a web server on the Ethernet shield so that it can be accessed from any device in your local network.

Chapter 4, *Controlling Objects from Anywhere*, covers how to connect a relay module to our Arduino and Ethernet shield hardware so that it can be controlled via the network. We are first going to control this relay module from within your local network, and then use a dedicated service to be able to control this relay from anywhere. As an example, we are also going to connect a lamp to this relay module.

Chapter 5, *Internet of Things with Xively*, continues with cloud-connected projects by interfacing the Ethernet shield with a cloud service called Xively. Using this service, we will be able to send the data measured by our project to the Web and monitor it in real time from the Xively website, from anywhere in the world.

Chapter 6, *Logging Data in Google Docs*, uses the web service Temboo to interface the Ethernet shield with even more web services such as Google Docs or Gmail. For example, we are going to make measurements using our Arduino board and automatically log these results in a Google Docs spreadsheet, which can be accessed from anywhere in the world.

What you need for this book

You will need several hardware and software components to make all the projects found in this book. Of course, you can just read the description of the projects and learn this way. However, I really recommend actually doing the projects yourself to really learn about how to use the Arduino Ethernet shield to build exciting networking applications.

The hardware components required are detailed at the beginning of each chapter. However, what you will really need for all the projects is an Arduino board.

All the projects of the book are based on the Arduino Uno board:

http://arduino.cc/en/Main/arduinoBoardUno

For all the projects of this book, you will also need the Arduino Ethernet shield:

http://arduino.cc/en/Main/ArduinoBoardEthernet

On the software side, there is some software that we will use in all the chapters of the book. The first software that we will use in all the chapters is the Arduino IDE that you need to install. You can download it from:

http://arduino.cc/en/main/software

The Ethernet library itself is contained within the Arduino IDE, so you won't need to install it yourself. There are also several external libraries you will need, but these are detailed in each chapter where they are necessary.

You will also need a web server running on your computer for some of the projects. I recommend using software that integrates a web server and a database, and that handles all the details for you.

If you are working on Windows, I recommend using EasyPHP:

http://www.easyphp.org/

Under OS X, I recommend using MAMP:

http://www.mamp.info/

For Linux, you can follow the instructions provided at the following link to install a web server:

http://doc.ubuntu-fr.org/lamp

Make sure that the server is running at this point; we are going to use it in several projects in this book.

Who this book is for

This book is for all those who are willing to build exciting connected Arduino projects using the Ethernet shield. You actually don't need to know the Arduino platform beforehand as all the projects will be explained step by step with clear instructions. You also don't need any prior knowledge in the Ethernet technology. The only thing you need to understand is the projects found in this book are just basic knowledge in electronics and programming.

This book is also for electronic hobbyists who want to learn more about the Arduino platform. By executing the projects found in this book, you will learn about many possible ways to use the Arduino Ethernet shield. You will also learn how to connect sensors and actuators to Arduino and control them within your local network.

Finally, this book is also for those who are willing to learn more about the Internet of Things framework using the Arduino Ethernet shield. The last chapters of the book are dedicated to building projects that are connected to cloud services and can be accessed from anywhere in the world, simply by connecting your Arduino projects to your Internet router via Ethernet.

Conventions

In this book, you will find a number of styles of text that distinguish between different kinds of information. Here are some examples of these styles and an explanation of their meaning.

Code words in text, database table names, folder names, filenames, file extensions, pathnames, dummy URLs, user input, and Twitter handles are shown as follows: "In the `setup()` function of the sketch, we will try to get an IP address using DHCP."

A block of code is set as follows:

```
String log_time = String(day()) + "/" +
String(month()) + "/" + String(year()) + " " +
String(hour()) + ":" + String(minute()) + ":" +
String(second());
```

Any command-line input or output is written as follows:

```
# 192.168.1.103/digital/7/1
```

New terms and **important words** are shown in bold. Words that you see on the screen, in menus or dialog boxes for example, appear in the text like this: "If you are using Windows, you will find the information you need under **Network Settings** in your **Control Panel**."

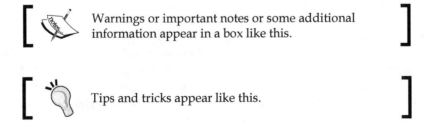

[Warnings or important notes or some additional information appear in a box like this.]

[Tips and tricks appear like this.]

Reader feedback

Feedback from our readers is always welcome. Let us know what you think about this book—what you liked or may have disliked. Reader feedback is important for us to develop titles that you really get the most out of.

To send us general feedback, simply send an e-mail to feedback@packtpub.com, and mention the book title through the subject of your message.

If there is a topic that you have expertise in and you are interested in either writing or contributing to a book, see our author guide on www.packtpub.com/authors.

Customer support

Now that you are the proud owner of a Packt book, we have a number of things to help you to get the most from your purchase.

Downloading the example code

You can download the example code files for all Packt books you have purchased from your account at http://www.packtpub.com. If you purchased this book elsewhere, you can visit http://www.packtpub.com/support and register to have the files e-mailed directly to you.

All the up-to-date code for the projects of this book can also be found at the following address:

https://github.com/openhomeautomation/arduino-networking/

Errata

Although we have taken every care to ensure the accuracy of our content, mistakes do happen. If you find a mistake in one of our books—maybe a mistake in the text or the code—we would be grateful if you would report this to us. By doing so, you can save other readers from frustration and help us improve subsequent versions of this book. If you find any errata, please report them by visiting http://www.packtpub.com/support, selecting your book, clicking on the **errata submission form** link, and entering the details of your errata. Once your errata are verified, your submission will be accepted and the errata will be uploaded to our website, or added to any list of existing errata, under the Errata section of that title.

Piracy

Piracy of copyright material on the Internet is an ongoing problem across all media. At Packt, we take the protection of our copyright and licenses very seriously. If you come across any illegal copies of our works, in any form, on the Internet, please provide us with the location address or website name immediately so that we can pursue a remedy.

Please contact us at copyright@packtpub.com with a link to the suspected pirated material.

We appreciate your help in protecting our authors, and our ability to bring you valuable content.

Questions

You can contact us at questions@packtpub.com if you are having a problem with any aspect of the book, and we will do our best to address it.

1
Discover the Arduino Ethernet Shield

In this first chapter of the book, we will only focus on the basics and get started with the Arduino Ethernet shield. In order to build more complex projects in the next chapters of the book, we first need to be absolutely sure that our shield is functioning correctly, and it can connect to our local network and the Web.

To ensure this, we'll first assemble the hardware, and then build a simple Arduino sketch that will connect to the Web, grab a test web page, and display it back inside the Arduino Serial Monitor.

These will be the major takeaways of this chapter:

- First, we'll make sure that you have all the required hardware and software components. We are also going to assemble the shield and the Arduino Uno board, and connect everything to our local network via a router.

- Then, we will write the sketch that will connect your shield to your local network as well as the Web, and this sketch will grab a test page to make sure your connection is working correctly.

- Finally, we are going to test this sketch and monitor the status of the Ethernet shield on the Arduino Serial Monitor. From this first test of the shield, we'll be able to tell whether the shield is correctly connected to the Internet or not.

Hardware and software requirements

You don't need a lot of hardware for this first project. You only need an Arduino Uno board, and of course, the Arduino Ethernet shield. Other boards such as the Arduino Mega will work as well for the projects in the first chapter of the book, but you might face difficulties for the projects in the following chapters in the book. Therefore, I recommend that you use an Arduino Uno board for all the projects of this book.

Before actually assembling the shield with the board, make sure to write down the MAC address of the shield, which is written on the back of the shield. We will need it later in the project when we write the first sketch.

This is an image of the assembled board and the Ethernet shield:

You will also need a USB B to USB A cable to connect the Arduino board to your computer, and an Ethernet cable to connect the shield to a router.

On the software side, all you need is the Arduino IDE, which can be found at the following address:

http://arduino.cc/en/main/software

The Ethernet library is included by default in the Arduino software, so you don't need to install any additional components.

Hardware configuration

The hardware configuration in this chapter is really simple. At this point, you should already have the Arduino Ethernet shield connected to your Arduino Uno board. If that's not the case, please do so now.

You then have only two cables to plugin: a USB cable between your computer and the Arduino Uno board and the Ethernet cable. Simply connect the USB cable to one port of your computer.

For the Ethernet cable, you have several options. The easiest thing you can do, which is what I recommend, is to connect the Ethernet cable directly from the shield to the main router of your home. Usually, you will have a Wi-Fi router in your home, which you use to enable Wi-Fi connectivity for your computer and other devices. This router should also have some Ethernet ports, where you can connect your Ethernet shield. The advantage of this solution is that your shield will automatically get an IP address and will have access to the Internet automatically. This assumes that your router is configured for DHCP; go to your router settings to enable DHCP. As this procedure varies depending on the brand of your router, refer to your router documentation to find out how to do this on your specific router.

If you don't have a router, you can directly connect the Ethernet cable to your computer. I don't recommend this alternative, as configuring your computer to connect to the shield and sharing the Internet connection with the shield is really complex, and it also depends on your operating system.

If you really don't have access to a router but you have access to a Wi-Fi network, I recommend buying one of these small Wi-Fi routers that have an Ethernet port. It can connect to any Wi-Fi network in range and share the connection automatically with other devices via Ethernet.

For example, as shown in the following image, I recommend the *TP-Link MR3020 router*:

This is an image of the assembled hardware for the tasks in this chapter, with the USB cable and the Ethernet cable plugged in the project:

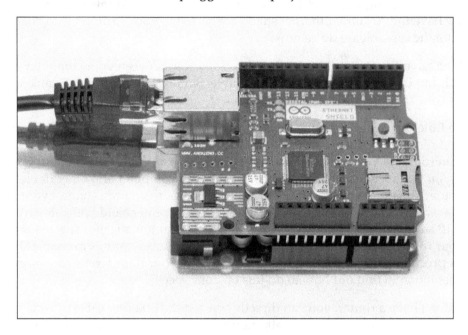

If everything is wired correctly, you should see the **ON** LED on the Ethernet shield is switched on, as well as the **LINK** LED near the Ethernet port.

Testing your connection

Now that the hardware is ready, we can write our first sketch to test the Ethernet shield and the connection to the Web. Note that the pieces of code shown in this section are only the most important parts of the code, and you can find the complete code inside the GitHub repository of the book.

Start the Arduino sketch by including the following required libraries to use the shield:

```
#include <SPI.h>
#include <Ethernet.h>
```

Downloading the example code

You can download the example code files for all Packt books you have purchased from your account at http://www.packtpub.com. If you purchased this book elsewhere, you can visit http://www.packtpub.com/support and register to have the files e-mailed directly to you.

Then, we have to define the MAC address of the Ethernet shield. This address is located just behind the shield, and you should have noted it down already. You have to enter it in the following format:

```
byte mac[] = { 0x90, 0xA2, 0xDA, 0x0E, 0xFE, 0x40 };
```

We also need to define where we are going to connect to test the connection. You can use any web page you want, or even perform a search on Google, but for this first test, I want to use a simple page.

I found this website with a simple test page that we'll try to grab while making a request later in the sketch. You can also set up your own page if you have a web server online, for example, if you have a blog hosted somewhere.

The website address is stored in a char variable:

```
char server[] = "www.brainjar.com";
```

Note that you can also use other pages here, for example http://www.example.com/hello.

The Ethernet shield will then automatically get the IP address of this website.

To get an IP address for the Ethernet shield itself, we'll use DHCP to automatically get one from the router we are connected to. However, if DHCP fails, we need to assign a default address to the shield.

This is stored in an IPAddress variable. Note that you can put anything you want inside this variable. As for this first project, we really need DHCP to work to get connected to the Web. However, it is a good practice to specify an IP address in the same subnet as your router, so the shield can at least connect to your local network. For example, the IP address of my computer was 192.168.1.100, so I specified a similar IP address for the shield:

```
IPAddress ip(192,168,1,50);
```

We can now create the instance for the Ethernet client with the following code:

```
EthernetClient client;
```

Now, in the `setup()` function of the sketch, we will try to get an IP address using DHCP. If you're connected to a router, there is no reason it would fail. However, if it does indeed fail, we will automatically set the default IP address for the shield:

```
if (Ethernet.begin(mac) == 0) {
    Serial.println("Failed to configure Ethernet using DHCP");
    Ethernet.begin(mac, ip);
}
```

Then, we will print out the IP address on the `Serial` port for debugging reasons:

```
Serial.begin(115200);
Serial.print("IP address: ");
Serial.println(Ethernet.localIP());
```

Now, in the `loop()` function of the sketch, we will actually connect to the server. It starts by calling the `connect` function and checks whether we are indeed connected. If that's the case, we print it out on the `Serial` monitor for debugging purposes:

```
if (client.connect(server, 80)) {
    if (client.connected()) {
        Serial.println("connected");
```

Now that we are connected, we can set the GET request for the test page we want to access:

```
client.println("GET /java/host/test.html HTTP/1.1");
client.println("Host: www.brainjar.com");
client.println("Connection: close");
client.println();
```

After the request is sent, we will read the data that is coming back from the server, to check whether everything went fine. We will also print out this data on the `Serial` monitor:

```
while (client.connected()) {
  while (client.available()) {
    char c = client.read();
    Serial.print(c);
  }
}
```

Finally, when we are sure that the client is not connected anymore, we will print the information on the `Serial` monitor and call the `close()` function on the Ethernet client:

```
if (!client.connected()) {
    Serial.println();
```

```
    Serial.println("disconnecting.");
    client.stop();
}
```

Finally, we don't want to continuously do this action, but only repeat it every five seconds. This is done with a `delay()` function:

```
delay(5000);
```

It's now time to test the sketch.

 The complete code for this first chapter can be found the GitHub repository of the book:

https://github.com/openhomeautomation/arduino-networking/tree/master/chapter1

Make sure that the Ethernet cable is plugged in your shield and your router, and upload the sketch to the Arduino board. You can now also open the Serial Monitor, and select the correct Serial speed (115200 for the Arduino sketch of this chapter); that's the first thing you should see, which is the IP address of your board:

IP address: 192.168.1.103

Then, the Arduino board should connect to the server:

Connecting...

If this is successful, the output will show that it is indeed connected:

connected

Now, the Arduino board will send the GET request to the server in order to grab the content of the test page. The server will answer with an HTTP 200 OK status if the request was successful, along with the contents of the page:

HTTP/1.1 200 OK

Content-Length: 308

Content-Type: text/html

Last-Modified: Tue, 27 May 2003 15:17:04 GMT

Accept-Ranges: bytes

ETag: "6291ea76324c31:5897"

Server: Microsoft-IIS/6.0

X-Powered-By: ASP.NET

Date: Thu, 15 May 2014 17:35:40 GMT

Connection: close

Inside this long answer, you should see many HTML tags, such as `<html>` and `<head>` tags. Inside the answer, you should also get the content of the page inside a `<p>` tag as follows:

```
<p>This is a very simple HTML file.</p>
```

If you can see this, congratulations! Your Ethernet shield is working correctly! Finally, the Arduino board will also display that the Ethernet shield has been disconnected from the remote server:

```
disconnecting
```

If everything worked correctly, it means that your Ethernet shield is working correctly, and it can connect without any problems to your local network and to the Web.

If something didn't work as expected, there are several things you can check. First, make sure that all connections are correctly made, and that the Ethernet cable is correctly plugged between the shield and your router.

If the DHCP fails at the beginning of the sketch and your shield can't get an IP address, please check whether DHCP is activated without limitations on the MAC addresses in the configuration panel of your router.

Finally, if the Arduino board can't connect to the remote server, first check whether the server itself is working by entering the URL of the test page manually in your browser.

Summary

In this first chapter of the book, we built our first project with the Arduino Ethernet shield, only to check whether the shield was working correctly and whether it could connect to your local network and to the Internet. We only made sure that the Ethernet shield could indeed be connected to the Internet, but this already gave you an overview of everything that you can do with the Ethernet shield. You saw how easy it is to send requests with the Ethernet shield, which is something we will use later in the book to send data from the Ethernet shield to a remote server.

These were the major takeaways from this first chapter:

- First, we made sure that all the hardware was correctly set and that the shield was connected to your router via an Ethernet cable.

- Then, we built the first sketch of this book simply to test that the Ethernet shield could indeed connect to the local network and the Web. To test this, we built a sketch that connects to the Web and grabs a test page from a remote server.

- Finally, we uploaded this code to the board and checked that everything was working correctly by monitoring the status of the connection in the Arduino Serial Monitor. We also defined some strategies on what to do if the sketch didn't work and the shield could not connect to the Web.

In the next chapter of the book, we are going to build our first application using the Ethernet shield. We are also going to use an Ethernet client, but this time to connect to a server running on our own computer and to send measurements that come from a temperature and humidity sensor.

2
Sending Data to a Web Server

In the previous chapter, we made sure that your Arduino Ethernet shield could actually connect to your local network and to the Web. In this chapter, we are going to build on that, and build our first application using the Ethernet shield.

We are going to see in more detail how the Ethernet client works by measuring data from a digital sensor and sending this data to a web server. In this chapter, this web server will be a server running on your own computer.

These will be the major takeaways from this chapter:

- First, we are going to choose the temperature and humidity sensor that we will also use later in the book. We are also going to install the different software components that are required for this chapter, especially the library to plot data on your computer.

- Then, we are going to build the Arduino code that will perform measurements and send these measurements to the web server running on your computer.

- After that, we'll start building the server-side code. In the first part, we are going to build the code responsible for simply logging the received data into a local database.

- Finally, we will interface the database with a live plotting library so the measurements can be seen as they come from the Ethernet shield and are logged in the database.

Hardware and software requirements

On the hardware side, you will of course need the Arduino Uno board and Arduino Ethernet shield.

You will also need a sensor to measure some data. As this book is about how to use the Ethernet shield and not how to measure data from sensors, you can actually take any sensor of your choice.

I used a DHT11 sensor, which is a digital temperature and humidity sensor. I chose this sensor for this chapter and for many chapters of the book since it is a very cheap sensor and easy to interface with Arduino. Along with the DHT11 sensor, you will also need a 4.7k Ohm resistor.

You can also use other kind of sensors. You can use analog sensors, which return a signal depending on the measured data. For example, the TMP36 sensor is an analog temperature sensor that returns a voltage proportional to the ambient temperature.

Other kind of sensors you can use here are sensors based on the SPI or I2C protocols, which are digital communication protocols that are easy to use with Arduino. For example, you can use the BMP085 or BMP180 sensors, which have an I2C interface, and you can also measure the barometric pressure and ambient humidity.

You will also need a breadboard and some jumper wires to make the connections between the sensor and the Ethernet shield.

This is a list of all the components that were used for this chapter:

- Arduino Uno (`https://www.adafruit.com/products/50`)
- Arduino Ethernet Shield (`https://www.adafruit.com/products/201`)
- DHT11 sensor (`https://www.adafruit.com/products/386`)
- Breadboard (`https://www.adafruit.com/product/64`)
- Jumper wires (`https://www.adafruit.com/product/758`)

On the software side, the first thing you will need is the library to interface with the sensor you chose before. As I chose a DHT11 sensor for this project, you will need to download and install the DHT library:

`https://github.com/adafruit/DHT-sensor-library`

To install an Arduino library, simply unzip the content of the downloaded file into the `/libraries` folder of your main Arduino folder (or create this folder if it doesn't exist already).

You will also need a library to plot the data stored in the database. I used the `flot` library, which is very convenient to use and allows real-time visualization of incoming data. This library is included in the code of this chapter, but if you want more information on the library you can go to `http://www.flotcharts.org/`.

About the database itself, this project uses SQLite, which is a lite and easy-to-use database. It is perfect for such projects, as it doesn't require a database server running on your computer.

It comes preinstalled on many operating systems such as OS X or Linux, but if that's not the case, go over to their website to download and install it:

`http://www.sqlite.org/`

If you are using Linux, the best option is to install SQLite with your Linux distribution package manager.

Note that it is also possible to use relational databases other than SQLite, such as MySQL. Many web servers come with the MySQL server as well, and you will only need to make small changes in the code of this chapter to use a MySQL database. You can also use nonrelational databases such as MongoDB (`http://www.mongodb.org/`), but this will require more changes in the code.

Finally, you will also need to have a web server up and running to make this project work. You can find more information about how to set up a web server in the preface of this book. If you don't have a web server installed yet, you can visit the following links to get one:

- Windows: EasyPHP (`http://www.easyphp.org/`) or WAMP (`http://www.wampserver.com/en/`)
- OS X: MAMP (`http://www.mamp.info/`)
- Linux: LAMP (`https://help.ubuntu.com/community/ApacheMySQLPHP`)

Hardware configuration

It's now time to set up the hardware for this project. At this point, if you followed the first chapter, you should already have your Arduino Ethernet shield plugged into the Arduino board, and one Ethernet cable connecting the Ethernet shield and your Internet router. If that's not the case already, please do so.

The only thing you will have to connect in this project is the DHT11 sensor and the resistor. You can have an overview of the different connections you have to make by looking at the following schematics:

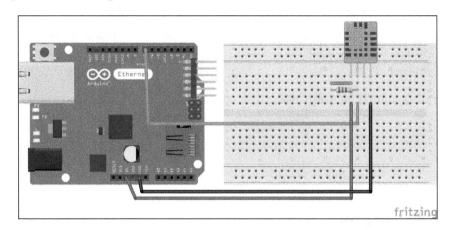

First, plug the DHT11 sensor to the breadboard. Then, connect pin number 1 and 2 of the sensor using the 4.7k Ohm resistor.

Now, for the power supply. Connect pin number 1 of the sensor to Arduino 5 V, and pin number 4 to the Arduino GND. Finally, connect pin number 2 of the DHT sensor to Arduino pin number 7.

This is what it should look like at the end:

If your project looks the same, congratulations, you can move to the next part where we are going to build the Arduino sketch for this project.

Sending data to a server

It is now time to build the sketch for our first application using the Arduino Ethernet shield. But first, we need one more piece of data: the local IP address of your computer. Inside the Arduino sketch, we are going to specify where the Arduino Ethernet shield has to send the data.

Finding your IP address is easy, but it depends on your operating system. If you are using OS X, you can find your IP address inside **Network Preferences**.

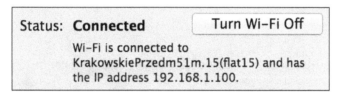

If you are using Windows, you will find the information you need under the **Network Settings** in your **Control Panel**:

Another way under Windows is to go to **Start**, then **Run**, and type cmd. Then, inside the console, type ipconfig and hit *Enter*. Your computer's IP address will be displayed.

If you are using Linux or OS X, you can simply go to a terminal and type:

```
ifconfig
```

This command should print your IP address inside the terminal window. It will in general be something like eth0 or en0. This is what I had on my machine:

```
en0: flags=8863<UP,BROADCAST,SMART,RUNNING,SIMPLEX,MULTICAST> mtu 1500
    ether b8:f6:b1:12:c4:d7
    inet6 fe80::baf6:b1ff:fe12:c4d7%en0 prefixlen 64 scopeid 0x4
    inet 192.168.1.100 netmask 0xffffff00 broadcast 192.168.1.255
```

```
nd6 options=1<PERFORMNUD>
media: autoselect
status: active
```

Some Linux distributions made the move to another tool called `ip`. To use it, simply go to a terminal and type:

ip addr

This will also display your computer's IP address.

We are now ready to build the Arduino sketch. First, we need to include the required libraries:

```
#include <SPI.h>
#include <Ethernet.h>
#include "DHT.h"
```

Insert the MAC address of your Ethernet shield, which you can find on the back of the shield:

```
byte mac[] = { 0x90, 0xA2, 0xDA, 0x0E, 0xFE, 0x40 };
```

You will also need to define the pin on which the DHT sensor was connected, as well as the type of sensor you are using:

```
#define DHTPIN 7
#define DHTTYPE DHT11
```

Note that you do not need a sensor connected to your Arduino board to test this project. You can simply send the content of any variable as a test, or use the `random()` function of Arduino to generate random data measurements.

First, we will define a default IP address for the Ethernet shield. The sketch should not use this address since we'll attempt to connect using DHCP, but if DHCP fails, we need this default IP address. I recommend using an address that is in the same IP domain as your computer IP address:

```
IPAddress ip(192,168,1,50);
```

Then, we can define the IP address of the server, which in this case is your computer. This is where you need to enter the IP address you got before:

```
IPAddress server(192,168,1,100);
```

We can then create an instance of the Ethernet client:

```
EthernetClient client;
```

We can also create an instance of the DHT library:

```
DHT dht(DHTPIN, DHTTYPE);
```

Now in the `setup()` function of the sketch, we first try to use DHCP to automatically get an IP address for the Ethernet shield. This is done using the following piece of code:

```
Serial.begin(115200);
if (Ethernet.begin(mac) == 0) {
  Serial.println("Failed to configure Ethernet using DHCP");
  Ethernet.begin(mac, ip);
}
```

After this step, we print the IP address on the `Serial` port:

```
Serial.print("IP address: ");
Serial.println(Ethernet.localIP());
```

In the `loop()` function of the sketch, the first step is to take measurements from the DHT11 sensor:

```
float h = dht.readHumidity();
float t = dht.readTemperature();
```

Convert these measurements into strings:

```
String temp = String((int) t);
String hum = String((int) h);
```

For debugging purposes, we also print these values on the `Serial` port. We'll check later whether these values are correct when testing the sketch:

```
Serial.println("Temperature: " + temp);
Serial.println("Humidity: " + hum);
```

Now, we are actually going to send the data to the server. Don't worry about understanding what the server-side code does for now, as we'll deal with that later. First, we have to connect to the server running on your computer:

```
if (client.connect(server, 80)) {
  if (client.connected()) {
    Serial.println("connected");
```

If this is successful, we can make the request. As in *Chapter 1, Discover the Arduino Ethernet Shield*, we are going to use a standard GET request, and to pass the temperature and humidity measurements as arguments. At this point, you will also need to enter the IP address of your computer. This is all done using the following piece of code:

```
client.println("GET /datalogger/datalogger.php?temp=" + temp + "&hum="
+ hum + " HTTP/1.1");
  client.println("Host: 192.168.1.100");
  client.println("Connection: close");
  client.println();
```

You can see that the code calls a filename `datalogger.php`, which we are going to examine in the next section.

Then, after the request is made, we can read the answer from the server:

```
while (client.connected()) {
  while (client.available()) {
  char c = client.read();
  Serial.print(c);
  }
}
```

Next, we can close the connection if the client is not connected to the server anymore:

```
if (!client.connected()) {
  Serial.println();
    Serial.println("disconnecting.");
    client.stop();
  }
```

We are also going to repeat the whole loop every second:

```
delay(1000);
```

> You can find all the code for this section in the GitHub repository of this chapter:
>
> `https://github.com/openhomeautomation/arduino-networking/tree/master/chapter2`

Now, if we just uploaded the code to the Arduino board, not much would have happened, since we didn't do anything on the server side. The Arduino board would make the request, but as the request file doesn't exist on the server, the server would return an error code.

So first, we need to build a file on the server that will handle the request from the board and log the data somewhere. That's exactly what we are going to do next.

Log incoming data in a database

In this section, we are going to use PHP to build the server-side part of the project. If you are a complete novice in PHP, I recommend the following resource to learn the basics of the language:

```
http://php.net/manual/en/tutorial.php
```

First, we are going to see the content of the `datalogger.php` file. This file will handle the requests coming from the Arduino board, log the data in a database, and answer with a simple message. Note that this file has to be in a folder named `datalogger` on your web server. We will see the important parts of the code. To get the complete code for this section, please refer to the GitHub repository of the chapter. Note that all the PHP code should be between the `<php ... ?>` tags.

The file starts by receiving the data from the GET request sent by the Arduino Ethernet shield:

```
$temperature = intval($_GET["temp"]);
$humidity = intval($_GET["hum"]);
```

We also instantiate the connection with the SQLite database:

```
$db = new SQLite3('database.db');
```

Then, we need to give some structure to the database if the database file is brand new. If you are not familiar with the SQL commands, I invite you to visit the following link:

```
http://www.cs.utexas.edu/~mitra/csFall2013/cs329/lectures/sql.html
```

We are going to create four different columns inside the database: a unique ID that will be automatically incremented by SQLite, a timestamp to know when the measurement was made, and the temperature and humidity data. This is done using the following piece of code:

```
$db->exec('CREATE TABLE IF NOT EXISTS measurements (id INTEGER
PRIMARY KEY, timestamp TIMESTAMP DEFAULT CURRENT_TIMESTAMP NOT NULL,
temperature INTEGER, humidity INTEGER);');
```

Note that if you are using more sensors (for example, if you are also measuring the ambient light level), you can add more fields here. Simply add a new field to the list, for example: `pressure INTEGER`.

Now, we can actually insert the data as a new row in the database. Since SQLite automatically adds the ID and timestamp fields, we just need to insert the data concerning the temperature and humidity:

```
$db->exec("INSERT INTO measurements (temperature, humidity) VALUES
('$temperature', '$humidity');");
```

If you need to insert more data into the database, for example, if you have another measurement to log, you can simply extend this command to insert more data into the SQLite database.

This simple code illustrates how easy it is to insert data into the SQLite database. However, it leaves our server exposed to a security issue known as the SQL injection. Since our project is made for your own local network only, this is not really an issue here. However, if you plan to deploy the project online, I recommend modifying the code to solve this security problem. The following link will give you more information about this issue http://www.tutorialspoint.com/sqlite/sqlite_injection.htm.

Finally, we reply to the Arduino board with a simple message:

```
echo "Data received";
```

Now, we haven't actually talked about the database itself yet. There is a database.db file included as an example in the code for this chapter, but I recommend you simply delete it and try to make your own database. You can simply go to the directory in a terminal where all files of the project are located and type:

sqlite3 database.db

If you are using Windows, I recommend using Console as a terminal. You can get it at the following link http://sourceforge.net/projects/console/.

This command will create your database file. You can now again exit the database file by typing the following command:

.exit

Note that if you are under Linux, you might have to change the permissions on the database and the folder that contains the project. To do so, go the project's folder via a terminal and type:

chmod 777 database.db

Now, it is time to make a first test of the project. Make sure that all the files of the server are located in a folder called `datalogger` on your web server. You can now upload the Arduino sketch to your board and open the `Serial` monitor. You should first see that the sketch is connecting to your network and receiving an `IP address` as follows:

```
IP address: 192.168.1.103
```

Then, it should enter the first iteration of the `loop()` function, and print out the temperature and humidity measurements:

```
Temperature: 21
Humidity: 37
```

After this step, you should see that the sketch is connected to your server, and that the server is answering with a standard `200 OK` answer:

```
connected
HTTP/1.1 200 OK
Date: Mon, 19 May 2014 08:09:57 GMT
Server: Apache/2.2.23 (Unix) mod_ssl/2.2.23 OpenSSL/0.9.8y DAV/2
PHP/5.4.10
X-Powered-By: PHP/5.4.10
Content-Length: 13
Connection: close
Content-Type: text/html
```

Also, at the end of this answer, you should see the confirmation message that we defined in the PHP file:

```
Data received
disconnecting.
```

If you are seeing these messages, congratulations! It means that your Arduino Ethernet shield is successfully communicating with the web server running on your computer, and is actually logging some data.

If this is not the case, first check your hardware connections. Make sure the DHT11 sensor is correctly wired with the Arduino board, and that the Ethernet cable is plugged into the shield and your Internet router. Don't hesitate to redo *Chapter 1, Discover the Arduino Ethernet Shield*, to make sure that your Ethernet shield is working properly.

Also, make sure that the web server is active on your computer, and that all the files of the project (especially the `datalogger.php` file) are located in a folder named `datalogger` inside your web server folder. You can test this independently from the Arduino Ethernet shield. Simply go to your favorite web browser, and type:

```
localhost/folder_of_the_project/datalogger.php?temp=20&hum=40
```

This will log some fake data inside the database, so you can be sure that the web server is running correctly.

We are now going to check on the server side whether the data was recorded correctly. And we are actually going to kill two birds with one stone, since this code will also be used in the next section to plot the data.

To check that the data was recorded correctly, you can simply create a file named `readout.php`, which will read data from the database, format it, and print the formatted data so you that can see it. First, we need to access the SQLite database:

```
$db = new SQLite3('database.db');
```

We then need to make a query to the database so it returns the data we want. In this request, we are simply going to take all the fields from the table called measurements. This is done using the following piece of code:

```
$results = $db->query('SELECT id, timestamp, temperature, humidity
FROM measurements');
```

Now, we need to use PHP to parse this variable that contains all the results from the query. We simply use a while statement for that:

```
while($row = $results->fetchArray())
{
   $dataset[] = array(strtotime($row['timestamp']) *
1000,$row['temperature']);
}
```

Note that in the process of parsing the results, we format the data in another variable, so that the script we will use to plot the data can use it. We also convert the timestamp column so that the plotting script can use it. In this example, we are just going to display and later plot the temperature, which is why we only take these two variables out from the database. You can, of course, do the same for the humidity.

Finally, we print out the formatted data in the JSON format:

```
echo json_encode($dataset);
```

Now, we can test this readout file. Simply go over to a terminal, go to the folder where the file is located, and type:

```
php readout.php
```

This should plot all the recordings that have been made so far:

```
[[1400486855000,20],[1400486868000,20],[1400486879000,21],[1400486890000,
21],[1400486901000,21],[1400486912000,21],[1400486922000,22],[14004869330
00,23],[1400486944000,23]]
```

What are you are seeing in the terminal window is the raw data that was recorded for the temperature. It consists of several small arrays of two elements, which are the timestamp and recorded temperature. If you want to learn more about the JSON format that this PHP script is returning, you can visit http://json.org/.

If you can see this raw data being displayed, it means that the data coming from the Arduino board was correctly logged in your computer.

Displaying the results

We are now going to use the data that was logged in the database and display it on a graph for more convenience. For this task, we are going to use a JavaScript library called flot, which is already included in the code for this chapter. This library provides nice functions to plot data on a web page, and also allows you to plot data in real time, so you will see the graph being automatically updated as more data comes in.

Everything will happen inside an HTML file called plot.html. We will only see the most important parts of the code here. Please refer to the GitHub repository of the chapter to get the complete files. Inside this file, you first have to include the files required for the flot library:

```
<script src="flot/jquery.js"></script>
<script src="flot/jquery.flot.js"></script>
<script src="flot/jquery.flot.time.js"></script>
```

You also need an element in the HTML page that will host the graph. This is done using the following piece of code:

```
<div id="placeholder" style="width:800px; height:450px;"></div>
```

Let's also define some options for the plot. Since this is now JavaScript, we have to write this code inside the <script>...</script> tags. If you want to learn more about JavaScript first, I recommend this excellent interactive tutorial:

```
http://www.codecademy.com/en/tracks/javascript
```

Because we have timestamps as the *x-axis*, we need to specify that the data for this axis is a specific time, and that we want to display the hours, minutes, and seconds:

```
var options = {
  xaxis: {
    mode: "time",
    timeformat: "%H:%M:%S"
  }
};
```

We also need to receive the data every time we call the script to plot the data. This is done by an AJAX call to the PHP file we created before:

```
$.ajax({
  url: "readout.php",
  type: "GET",
  dataType: "json",
  success: onDataReceived
});
```

Note that this code has to go inside the `update()` function in the JavaScript code. You can define this function with:

```
function update() {
```

You can see that this AJAX call, if successful, calls another JavaScript function. This function will actually take the data as an argument and plot it with the options we defined before:

```
function onDataReceived(series) {
  var data = [];
  data.push(series);
  $.plot("#placeholder", data, options);
}
```

All this code is contained in the `update()` function, and this function is called continuously (every 10 milliseconds) so that the plot is always updated when a new data point comes in:

```
setTimeout(update, 10);
```

Finally, at the end of the script, we call this function once to get the graph started:

```
update();
```

It is now time to test the page we just created. Place all the files in the `datalogger` folder on your web server and make sure that the sketch is still loaded on the Arduino board.

For illustration purposes, I reset the measurement database at this point, but you can of course just keep the measurements that the sensor already performed.

Open the `plot.html` file. This is the result I got after the first two measurement points:

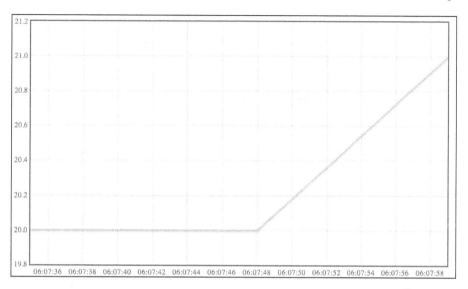

To illustrate the behavior of the sensor on the plot, I pinched it with my fingers and released it a bit later. As expected, the temperature went up before going down again after a while. The following screenshot is the result on the web page:

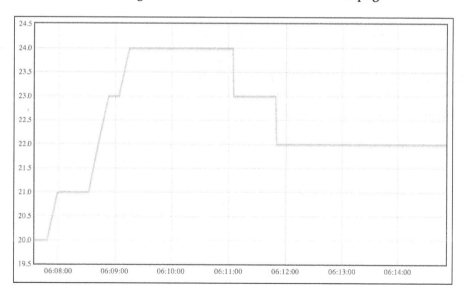

If it doesn't work at this point, there are many things you can check. First, make sure again that the code for the previous sections is working and that the Arduino Ethernet shield is correctly sending data to the server. Also, check that all the code files are located inside the same folder on the web server. And make sure that you are accessing plot.html via the localhost URL in your browser.

Then, open the JavaScript console to check that everything is fine. You will usually find the console in the developer tools of your web browser. For example, in Chrome, you will find the console in the View | Developer menu:

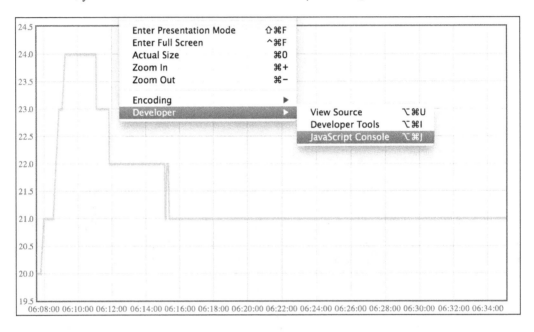

Inside this console, you will be able to see whether there are any errors in the JavaScript code on the page, and this will usually give you a good idea of what is going on in the page and what you have to fix.

Summary

In this second chapter of the book, we built our first application based on the Arduino Ethernet shield and Ethernet client class. We did some basic measurements on the Arduino board, sent these measurements on a local web server, and finally displayed this data in real time on a graph.

To proceed further with this chapter, I invite you to carefully repeat all the steps of this chapter to really understand well how the Arduino Ethernet shield communicates with the PHP code running on your computer. You can also add more sensors to the projects and log this data inside the database. Also, you can try to plot several variables at once on different graphs.

These were the major takeaways from this chapter:

- First, we interfaced a digital temperature and humidity sensor to the Arduino board so that we can send the measurements to a local web server using the Ethernet shield. We also installed some useful software components such as a library to plot data in a web page.

- Then, we built an Arduino sketch to send data directly to a web server running on your computer.

- After that, we started building the server-side code by coding the file responsible for logging data into a local database. We also tested this code with the Arduino Ethernet shield, and made sure that the data was correctly transmitted to the server and logged in the database.

- Finally, we built a web page to automatically plot the data as it is received on the web server, using a JavaScript library called `flot`.

In the next chapter, we are going to do similar things, but using a completely different approach: instead of running a client on the Arduino board and transmitting the data on a local web server, we are going to run the server right on the Arduino board. The Arduino project will constantly display the measurements on a web page and log the data locally on a SD card.

3
Data Logging Station

In this chapter, we are going to create something really similar to what we did in *Chapter 2*, *Sending Data to a Web Server*, that is measuring data from a sensor, storing the data, and sending it back to a web server so that it can be plotted.

However, things are going to be similar only on the appearance front. Instead of having an Ethernet client that runs on the Arduino board and sends data to a server, we are going to make the Arduino board more independent. In the first part of the chapter, we are going to log the data locally using the integrated MicroSD card reader of the Ethernet shield.

Then, we are going to create a server right on the Arduino board. The board will measure data as usual, but the server will serve the data to the incoming clients. Finally, we will use a modified version of the code we used in the *Chapter 2*, *Sending Data to a Web Server*, to plot the measured data on your computer.

The following will be the major takeaways of this chapter:

- First, we are going to build the hardware for this project, including the temperature and humidity sensor, and the SD card to log the measured data.

- Then, we will create the first part of the project, and log data automatically on the SD card, which is inserted inside the Ethernet shield. At this point, we are going to use the Internet connection of the Ethernet shield to automatically obtain the current time from a **Network Time Protocol (NTP)** time server.

- Finally, we are going to build a web server and run it on the Arduino board. You will then be able to access the data measured by the board just by entering in the address of the board in a web browser. We are also going to modify the code from the last chapter to obtain the measurements from the Arduino board and plot them live in your browser.

Hardware and software requirements

On the hardware front, you will of course, need the Arduino Ethernet shield and an Arduino board such as the Arduino Uno.

You will also need a sensor to measure some data. As this book is about how to use the Ethernet shield and not how to measure from sensors, you could actually take any sensor of your choice.

I used a DHT11 sensor, which is a digital temperature and humidity sensor. I chose this sensor for this chapter and for many chapters of the book as it is a very cheap sensor and easy to interface with Arduino. Along with the DHT11 sensor, you will also need a 4.7k ohm resistor.

To log the data, you will need to have a MicroSD card that you can plug into the Ethernet shield. I don't have a specific brand to recommend, but I used a SanDisk MicroSD card with a normal SD adapter (which worked well for me), so you can also plug it into your computer to check whether the data was correctly logged. Also, make sure that the SD card is formatted using the FAT32 format.

You will also need a breadboard and some jumper wires to create the connection between the sensor and the Ethernet shield.

The following is a list of all components that were used for this chapter:

- The Arduino Uno (https://www.adafruit.com/products/50)
- The Arduino Ethernet shield (https://www.adafruit.com/products/201)
- The DHT11 sensor (https://www.adafruit.com/products/386)
- A MicroSD card (http://www.amazon.com/SanDisk-Micro-SDHC-Memory-Adapter/dp/B0052MHQM6)
- A breadboard (https://www.adafruit.com/product/64)
- Jumper wires (https://www.adafruit.com/product/758)

On the software front, the first thing you will need is the library to interface with the sensor you chose before. I chose a DHT11 sensor for this project. You will need to download and install the DHT library from https://github.com/adafruit/DHT-sensor-library.

To install an Arduino library, simply unzip the content of the downloaded file to your `libraries` folder of your main Arduino folder (or create this folder if you haven't done so already).

Hardware configuration

It's now time to set up the hardware for this project. At this point, if you followed any of the previous chapters of this book, you should already have your Arduino Ethernet shield plugged into the Arduino board, and one Ethernet cable connecting the Ethernet shield and your Internet router. If that's not the case already, please do so.

The only thing you will have to connect in this project is the DHT11 sensor and the resistor. You can see an overview of the different connections you have to make by looking at the following schematic diagram:

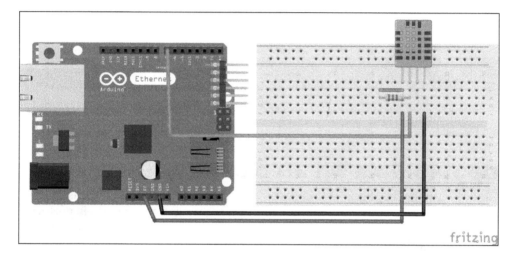

First, plug the DHT11 sensor into the breadboard. Then, connect the pin number 1 and 2 of the sensor using the 4.7k ohm resistor.

Now comes the power supply. Connect the pin number 1 of the sensor to the Arduino 5V, and the pin number 4 to the Arduino GND. Finally, connect the pin number 2 of the DHT sensor to the Arduino pin number 7.

At the end, it should look like the following image:

Finally, simply insert the SD card into the SD card slot on the Ethernet shield.

Logging data on an SD card

Let's start with the first topic of this chapter—logging data on a SD card using the integrated SD card slot of the Ethernet shield. What we are going to do is perform some measurements on the Arduino board and log each of these measurements to the SD card in a simple text file.

However, compared to the project of the *Chapter 2, Sending Data to a Web Server*, we don't actually know the date when the measurement was taken. In the previous chapter, we simply used the date of the computer, but we don't have this information here. To get the time on the Arduino board, we are going to use another strategy. We are going to use the Ethernet shield to connect to an NTP time server, grab the time once when the Arduino sketch starts, and then use the Time library to track the time from there.

To learn more about the Time library, you can visit the following page on the Arduino website:

```
http://playground.arduino.cc/Code/Time
```

The process of logging data on a SD card starts by including the correct libraries as follows:

```
#include "DHT.h"
#include <SD.h>
#include <Time.h>
#include <Ethernet.h>
#include <EthernetUdp.h>
#include <SPI.h>
```

We also need to define the sensor type and the pin to which the sensor is connected. This is done with the following lines of code:

```
#define DHTPIN 7
#define DHTTYPE DHT11
```

To define the MAC address of the Ethernet shield, use the following line of code:

```
byte mac[] = { 0x90, 0xA2, 0xDA, 0x0E, 0xFE, 0x40 };
```

To use the SD card, you will also need to define the chipSelect pin, which is the pin number 4 on the Ethernet shield. This is done using the following line:

```
const int chipSelect = 4;
```

Now, we are going to deal with the NTP server. There are actually several NTP servers you can use (you can see the IP addresses of many of these servers inside the TimeNTP example that come with the Time library). You can also set your time zone here. To get more information about which NTP server you can use and which time zone to set, you can have a look at the example TimeNTP sketch. This sketch is given as an example inside the Time library. For this project, I used the first server available with time zone number 1, as shown in the following code:

```
IPAddress timeServer(132, 163, 4, 101);
const int timeZone = 1;
```

To connect to this server, we also need to define an Ethernet client. This time, we are going to use a protocol different from the earlier one, which is called UDP. UDP is different from TCP—it's much simpler and lighter. However, it doesn't guarantee that the data was correctly delivered, which TCP does. You don't actually need to care about the details of this protocol, as the Time library handles everything. You can just leave the default UDP port, as shown in the following code:

```
EthernetUDP Udp;
unsigned int localPort = 8888;
```

You also need to create an instance of the DHT sensor as follows:

```
DHT dht(DHTPIN, DHTTYPE);
```

Now, in the `setup()` function of the sketch, you need to define the following code responsible for getting an IP address for the Ethernet shield:

```
Serial.begin(9600);
if (Ethernet.begin(mac) == 0) {
  // no point in carrying on, so do nothing forevermore:
  while (1) {
    Serial.println("Failed to configure Ethernet using DHCP");
    delay(10000);
  }
}
```

After that, we will try to initialize the SD card, as shown in the following code:

```
Serial.print("Initializing SD card...");
pinMode(10, OUTPUT);
```

If this is successful, we will print out a message on the `Serial` port, as shown in the following code:

```
if (!SD.begin(chipSelect)) {
  Serial.println("Card failed, or not present");
  // don't do anything more:
  return;
}
Serial.println("card initialized.");
```

We will also start the DHT sensor as follows:

```
dht.begin();
```

Finally, still in the `setup()` function, we will print out the IP address of the Ethernet shield and create the connection to the NTP server. Note that here we are calling a function called `getNtpTime`, which is defined later in the sketch. As this is a function provided by the `Time` library, we are not going to look into the details of this function. The following is the code for this part:

```
Serial.print("IP number assigned by DHCP is ");
Serial.println(Ethernet.localIP());
Udp.begin(localPort);
Serial.println("waiting for sync");
setSyncProvider(getNtpTime);
```

Now, in the `loop()` function of the sketch, we will first measure the temperature and humidity from the sensor using the following code:

```
float h = dht.readHumidity();
float t = dht.readTemperature();
```

Secondly, we will convert these measurements to strings as follows:

```
String temp = String((int) t);
String hum = String((int) h);
```

We are now going to build a string that contains the date and time of the measurement using the `Time` library. This library contains functions to get the current time, day, or month, for example, which are calculated from the initial call to the NTP server. For example, calling the `day()` function will return the current day. The following piece of code returns a string with the date and time:

```
String log_time = String(day()) + "/" +
String(month()) + "/" + String(year()) + " " +
String(hour()) + ":" + String(minute()) + ":" +
String(second());
```

We then assemble this string with the temperature and humidity measurements using commas as separators between the different strings, as shown in the following line of code:

```
String dataString = log_time + "," + temp + "," + hum;
```

We are now going to write this data on the SD card. We first need to open the card to write data using the following line:

```
File dataFile = SD.open("datalog.txt", FILE_WRITE);
```

If that's successful, we will put the contents of the `dataString` variable to this file named `datalog.txt`, as shown in the following code:

```
if (dataFile) {
  dataFile.println(dataString);
  dataFile.close();
  Serial.println(dataString);
}
else {
  Serial.println("error opening datalog.txt");
}
```

Finally, we will repeat the operation every 10 seconds, but you can, of course, modify this delay with the following line:

```
delay(10000);
```

 All the code for this section can be found inside the GitHub repository of this chapter at https://github.com/openhomeautomation/arduino-networking/tree/master/chapter3.

It's now time to test this sketch. Make sure that the Ethernet cable is plugged into the shield and your Internet router, and the SD card is plugged into the Ethernet shield SD card slot. You can now upload the sketch to the board and open the Serial Monitor. The following line is what you should see first:

```
Initializing SD card...card initialized.
```

Then, you should see that your Ethernet shield has an IP address, as shown in the following line:

```
IP number assigned by DHCP is 192.168.1.103
```

You should see that this shield is currently synchronizing the time with the NTP server, as shown in the following output:

```
waiting for sync
Transmit NTP Request
Receive NTP Response
```

After that, you should see that the first measurement is made as follows:

```
21/5/2014 9:32:13,22,38
```

After the delay you fixed in the sketch, you will see that a second measurement is made with the corresponding date and time. To be sure that the sketch is correctly writing data on the SD card, you can let it run for a while and then disconnect the Ethernet shield from the power supply. After this, remove the SD card, and read it on your computer via an adapter. You should see the following screenshot:

```
📄 DATALOG.TXT

                          21/5/2014 9:30:59,22,38
                          21/5/2014 9:31:10,22,38
                          21/5/2014 9:31:20,22,38
                          21/5/2014 9:31:31,22,38
                          21/5/2014 9:31:41,22,38
                          21/5/2014 9:31:52,22,38
                          21/5/2014 9:32:2,22,38
                          21/5/2014 9:32:13,22,38
                          21/5/2014 9:32:23,22,38
                          21/5/2014 9:32:34,22,38
                          21/5/2014 9:32:44,22,38
                          21/5/2014 9:32:55,22,38
                          21/5/2014 9:33:5,22,38
                          21/5/2014 9:33:16,22,38
                          21/5/2014 9:33:26,22,38
                          21/5/2014 9:33:37,22,38
                          21/5/2014 9:33:47,22,38
                          21/5/2014 9:33:58,22,38
```

As you can see, all the measurements were correctly logged on the SD card, and we can clearly see that the interval between two measurements was 10 seconds.

Creating a web server on Arduino

For the rest of this chapter, we are going to take another approach. We are still going to make the Arduino with the Ethernet Shield work as an independent system, but this time we are even going to create a web server on the Arduino board. This is actually similar to the project we saw in the *Chapter 2, Sending Data to a Web Server*, but this time it is the Arduino board itself that will display the data as it is measured.

The sketch for this part starts by including the right libraries, as shown in the following code:

```
#include "DHT.h"
#include <Ethernet.h>
#include <SPI.h>
```

Define the pin and the type of the sensor in the following manner:

```
#define DHTPIN 7
#define DHTTYPE DHT11
```

Also, you have to define the MAC address of your Ethernet shield as usual, as shown in the following line of code:

```
byte mac[] = { 0x90, 0xA2, 0xDA, 0x0E, 0xFE, 0x40 };
```

We will also define a default IP address in case the DHCP fails, as shown in the following line:

```
IPAddress ip(192,168,1,50);
```

This is where the new feature comes in. So far, we only used the `EthernetClient` class to define a client that will connect to a remote server. Here, however, because we want to create a server right on the Arduino board, we are going to use the `EthernetServer` class, as shown in the following line of code:

```
EthernetServer server(80);
```

You can use the port `80` for your server, as it will be much easier to access the server from your web browser.

We also should not forget to create an instance of the DHT sensor. This is done using the following line:

```
DHT dht(DHTPIN, DHTTYPE);
```

Now, in the `setup()` function of the sketch, we will try to use DHCP to get an IP address for the Ethernet shield using the following code:

```
if (Ethernet.begin(mac) == 0) {
  Serial.println("Failed to configure Ethernet using DHCP");
  Ethernet.begin(mac, ip);
}
```

Still in the `setup()` function, we also have to start our Ethernet server, and print out the IP address of the server using the following code:

```
server.begin();
Serial.print("Server is at ");
Serial.println(Ethernet.localIP());
```

Finally, we will start the DHT sensor as follows:

```
dht.begin();
```

Now, in the `loop()` part of the sketch, we will perform the temperature and humidity measurements, as shown in the following code:

```
float h = dht.readHumidity();
float t = dht.readTemperature();
```

Convert the measurements to strings using the following code:

```
String temp = String((int) t);
String hum = String((int) h);
```

Then, we need to handle the connections that come to the Arduino board, for example, from a web browser. To do so, we are actually going to create an instance of the `EthernetClient` class every time the server becomes available. As this is a class we already saw in previous chapters of the book, this is something we already know how to work with.

If a connection is detected, we create this client, and print it out on the `Serial` port for debugging purposes, as shown in the following code:

```
EthernetClient client = server.available();
if (client) {

    Serial.println("New client");
```

The next part is a bit technical. We need to read out the request that comes from the client, but also detect the moment when the request is over so that we can close the connection. This is handled by always checking whether the current line is blank or not. The first step is then to read out the request that comes from the client, character per character, using the following piece of code:

```
boolean currentLineIsBlank = true;
while (client.connected()) {

    // Read data
    if (client.available()) {
      char c = client.read();
        Serial.write(c);
```

Note that the incoming request is also printed out on the `Serial` port for debugging purposes. Now, if we detect that we have an end of line character and that the current line is blank, it's a sign that the request is over, as shown in the following line:

```
if (c == '\n' && currentLineIsBlank) {
```

Therefore, we can answer the client. We will first send a standard HTTP header that states everything went OK, and that we want to refresh the page automatically every 5 seconds, as shown in the following code:

```
client.println("HTTP/1.1 200 OK");
client.println("Content-Type: text/html");
client.println("Connection: close");
client.println("Refresh: 5");  // Refresh the page automatically
every 5 sec
client.println();
client.println("<!DOCTYPE HTML>");
client.println("<html>");
```

Then, we will print out the data from the measurement on the page using the following code:

```
client.print("Temperature: ");
client.print(temp);
client.print("<br />");
client.print("Humidity: ");
client.print(hum);
client.println("<br/>");
client.println("</html>");
```

The rest of the following code is there to detect whether we reached the end of the request or not:

```
if (c == '\n') {
  // Starting a new line
  currentLineIsBlank = true;
}
else if (c != '\r') {
  // you've gotten a character on the current line
  currentLineIsBlank = false;
}
```

Finally, we will give the browser a small delay to receive the answer, and we will close the connection, as shown in the following code:

```
// Give the web browser time to receive the data
delay(1);

// Close the connection:
client.stop();
Serial.println("Client disconnected");
```

All the code for this section can be found in the GitHub repository of this chapter at `https://github.com/openhomeautomation/arduino-networking/tree/master/chapter3`.

It's now time to test the code that we wrote in this section. Again, make sure that the Ethernet cable is plugged to the Ethernet shield and to your router. Then, you can upload the code to the board, and open the Serial Monitor. You should first see the IP address of the web server running on the Arduino board as follows:

```
Server is at 192.168.1.103
```

After that, the sketch will just do nothing while waiting for any incoming connection. To make a connection happen, just go over to your web browser and type in the IP address of the board. You should immediately see the GET request from the browser being printed out in the Arduino Serial Monitor, as shown in the following output:

```
New client
GET / HTTP/1.1
Host: 192.168.1.103
Connection: keep-alive
Cache-Control: max-age=0
Accept: text/html,application/xhtml+xml,application/xml;q=0.9,image/
webp,*/*;q=0.8
User-Agent: Mozilla/5.0 (Macintosh; Intel Mac OS X 10_9_3)
AppleWebKit/537.36 (KHTML, like Gecko) Chrome/34.0.1847.137 Safari/537.36
Referer: http://192.168.1.103/
Accept-Encoding: gzip,deflate,sdch
Accept-Language: fr-FR,fr;q=0.8,en-US;q=0.6,en;q=0.4,de;q=0.2
```

As we can see, there is a lot of text and this depends on your browser. However, the important thing is actually the first line of the request, which means it's a GET request to our Arduino board.

Finally, after the Arduino answers the server, the connection is closed and the following message is displayed:

```
Client disconnected
```

In your browser, you should also directly see that the data is being printed out on the page created by the Arduino board, as shown in the following screenshot:

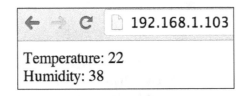

If you can see this, congratulations, you just created your own web server that runs on an Arduino board. If you can't see a page, first make sure that Arduino has an IP address and it can be connected to your local network. To do so, repeat the instructions in *Chapter 1, Discover the Arduino Ethernet Shield*, again.

Also make sure that you correctly entered the IP address of the board in your browser. You can also check on the Serial Monitor that you are not receiving any error messages from the DHT sensor, which will compromise the behavior of the web server.

Plotting the data locally

To end the chapter, we are going to see how to plot data measured by the Arduino board. To do so, we will modify the Arduino sketch a little bit, and then use part of the code from the previous chapter to plot the data right in your web browser.

First, we are going to modify the Arduino sketch so that it returns data in a more useful format; in the present case, the JSON format. In place of the code responsible to print out the measurements, we are going to simply print the data in the JSON format. This is done using the following piece of code:

```
client.println("HTTP/1.1 200 OK");
client.println("Content-Type: application/json");
client.println("Connection: close");
client.println();
client.print("{\"temperature\": ");
client.print(temp);
client.print(", \"humidity\": ");
client.print(hum);
client.println("}");
```

We can now quickly test this project. Upload the code to the Arduino board again, open your web browser, and go to the same IP address you used before. You should see the following line printed on the page:

```
{"temperature": 24, "humidity": 36}
```

Now, we also have to build the server-side code to plot the data. The code is very similar to the code of the previous chapter, so I will only detail the differences between the two projects. In the previous chapter, it was the board that was trying to reach out the server running on your computer, and the `datalogger.php` file was handling the requests. In this chapter, we are going to do the reverse and call the board from the web server running on your computer. To do so, we are going to use a module from PHP called cURL to make GET requests to a given URL; in this case, the URL of the Arduino board.

The first thing we have to do is make changes to the `datalogger.php` file and add the URL of the Arduino board, as shown in the following line of code:

```
$url = 'http://192.168.1.103';
```

Start the cURL call, as shown in the following line of code:

```
$curl = curl_init();
```

We also have to set the options of the cURL call. We want the call to return the data from our Arduino web server, and we also want the URL to be the one we defined before. This is done using the following code:

```
curl_setopt_array($curl, array(
    CURLOPT_RETURNTRANSFER => 1,
    CURLOPT_URL => $url,
));
```

We can now execute the command, as shown in the following line of code::

```
$resp = curl_exec($curl);
```

Close the cURL call, as follows:

```
curl_close($curl);
```

We get the answer in a variable that contains the data in a string. In order to open it with PHP, we need to convert it to the JSON format first, and then extract the temperature and humidity fields. This is done using the following piece of code:

```
$json = json_decode($resp, true);
$temperature = intval($json["temperature"]);
$humidity = intval($json["humidity"]);
```

The rest of the file is strictly identical to the code we developed in the previous chapter.

Now, we also need to make a small modification in the `plot.html` file. In the previous chapter, the data was automatically logged inside the database as the Arduino board was constantly sending data to the server. Here, we need to make the call on the server side. This is done by adding the following small piece of code just before the code that reads out the data from the database:

```
$.ajax({
    url: "datalogger.php",
    type: "GET",
});
```

This means that just before the data is read from the database to be plotted, we are calling the Arduino board to get the temperature and humidity measurements.

 All the code for this section can be found inside the GitHub repository of this chapter at `https://github.com/openhomeautomation/arduino-networking/tree/master/chapter3`.

We can now test this part of the chapter. Note that the code from the GitHub repository includes an example database so you can test the project right away, but I recommend deleting the file just before testing the project, so you will plot your own measured data while testing the code.

You can just put all the code for the plotting part inside a folder at the root of your web server. Then, open the `plot.html` file via the localhost URL in your web server. You should immediately see that data is being plotted inside your web browser. After a while, you should get a graph similar to the following graph:

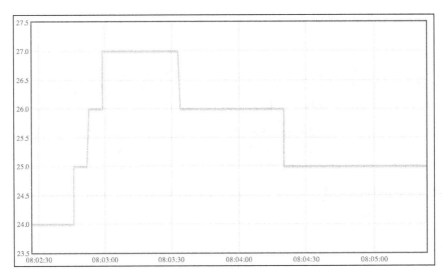

If you can see this plot in your browser, congratulations! This means you can perform remote measurements from the web server running on your Arduino board.

If this is not the case, there are several things you can check. This first thing you can check is making sure that the Arduino board correctly displays the data in a JSON format. To do so, you can simply enter the address of your board in a browser. Then, check whether your web server is running on your computer and that you have placed all the files from the project inside a repository in your web server's main folder. Finally, make sure that you are accessing the HTML file from the localhost URL in your browser and not by clicking on it inside your file explorer.

Summary

Let's summarize what we did in this chapter. We created an independent measurement station with Arduino that automatically measures and serves the data in some way. First, we logged the data locally on a SD card and then we served this data using a web server running on the Arduino board.

The following are the major takeaways of this chapter:

1. First, we built the required hardware for this chapter, and inserted the SD card into the Ethernet shield.

2. Then, in the first part of the project, we logged the measured data on the SD card and used a remote time server to automatically get the measurement times.

3. Finally, we built a new Arduino sketch to have a web server running on the Arduino board. We then modified the plotting code from the previous chapter so it can call the server on the Arduino board to get and plot the measured data.

There are, of course, many ways to improve this project. You can add more sensors to the project and either log this additional data on a SD card or serve it on a web page using the Arduino web server. You can also have many of these boards in your home or even outside and make your computer poll all these Arduino servers at a regular interval to get their measurements.

In the next chapter, we are going to work again with this idea of creating an independent system with the Arduino Ethernet shield. We are going to connect a relay to the Arduino board, so you can switch a lamp on and off remotely. This project will come in two flavors. First, we will make a sketch to control the relay remotely via your web browser. In the second part of the chapter, we will use a special library so the relay can be controlled from anywhere in the world.

4
Controlling Objects from Anywhere

In this chapter, we are going to do something different to what we did in the other chapters. What we did so far was measure some data on the Arduino board and transmit this data back to the network using the Ethernet shield. In this chapter, we are going to control a device instead of measuring data.

To do so, we will use a relay connected to the Arduino board with the Ethernet shield and control this relay remotely. We are also going to connect a set of power cables to this relay so you can directly plug a lamp into it so that it can be controlled remotely.

In the first part of the chapter, we are going to control this relay remotely within your local network. In the second part of the chapter, we will use a dedicated web service to control this relay from anywhere in the world.

The following will be the major takeaways from this chapter:

- First, we are going to see how to choose the different components for this project, including the relay and cables to connect a device to the relay such as a lamp.

- Then, we will assemble the different hardware components, connect the relay to the Arduino board, and the power cables to the relay.

- After that, we will write an Arduino sketch to test whether the relay is working correctly and has been correctly connected to the circuit.

- When we are sure that the relay is working, we will write an application using the Ethernet shield along with the relay. We are going to write a sketch to control the relay via Ethernet and then build an interface to control the relay from your web server.

- Finally, in the last section of the chapter, we are going to use a dedicated web service to control the relay from anywhere in the world. We are also going to adapt the interface we just created to control the relay from anywhere.

Hardware and software requirements

Let's first see what we need for this project. As with all the other chapters, you will need an Arduino board and the Arduino Ethernet shield.

You will also need a relay module. I really recommend using a relay that is integrated on a board, with all the required components on the board as well. It will avoid you having to build your own relay module on a breadboard, and it is also much safer. Indeed, there is no risk in wiring the relay and other components in an incorrect fashion. Simply make sure that the relay you choose is compatible with 5 V input voltage levels. Also, you have to make sure that the relay module can handle the power of the device you are going to use for this project. For example, the lamp I used was a 30 W lamp, and the relay could handle more than 1000 W, just to be on the safe side. I chose a 5 V relay module from Polulu, as shown:

You can simply use the relay as it is and control it with the code we are going to develop in this project, but the goal of having a relay is to connect a device to it. For this project, I chose to connect a lamp to the relay, but by following the instructions in this chapter, you will be able to connect any device that uses a standard power plug.

To do so, I used a set of power cables, one with a male socket and one with a female socket, as shown in the following image:

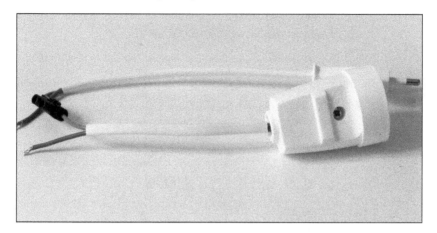

The male plug will be used to connect the relay to the main power plug in the wall and the female socket will be used to connect the device to control the relay.

Always be very careful when connecting wires to the main electricity. Make sure that you don't touch any of the exposed parts of the relay, and make sure that the cables themselves don't have any exposed copper. Also, connect the plug to the electricity latest when assembling the project.

Let's now see the software requirements for this project. As usual, you will need to have the Arduino IDE installed, along with a web server running on your computer.

In the second part of the chapter, we are going to use a service called Teleduino to control the Ethernet shield from anywhere. To use this service, you will need to get an API key, which you will have to insert inside the Arduino sketch.

You can get a key by visiting the following address:

```
https://www.teleduino.org/tools/request-key
```

You will be taken to the following page where you can get your key:

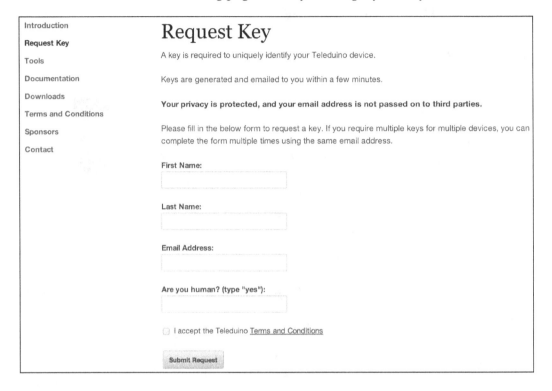

You will also need to install a few Arduino libraries for this chapter.

The first one you will need is the aREST library for Arduino, which you can find at the following link:

https://github.com/marcoschwartz/aREST

Finally, you will also need to download and install the Teleduino library, which you can find here:

https://www.teleduino.org/downloads/

To install a given library, simply extract the folder to your Arduino/libraries folder (or create this folder if it doesn't exist yet).

Hardware configuration

Now let's see how to connect the different components of the project. As with the other chapters of the book, you will need to have the Ethernet shield plugged into the Arduino board. You will also need to connect an Ethernet cable between the Ethernet shield and your router.

Then, you need to connect the relay module. The relay module has three input pins: **VCC, GND,** and a signal pin usually called **SIG**. You need to connect the VCC pin to Arduino 5 V, GND to Arduino GND, and finally the signal pin to Arduino pin number 7, which is a digital pin. The following image shows the system at this point:

Then, you need to connect the power cables to the relay module. A relay module basically has three output pins: **COM** (for the common pin), **NC** (for the normally closed pin), and **NO** (for the normally open pin).

What we want is to have the **COM** pin of the relay connected to one wire of the power plug, **NC** not connected, and **NO** connected to one other wire of the power plug. The following image summarizes the connections at this stage:

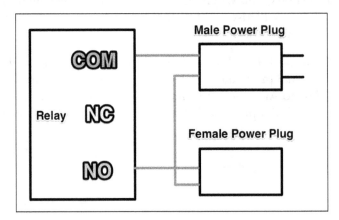

First, connect one pin of the female power plug to the **COM** pin. Then, connect one pin of the male power plug to the **NO** pin. Finally, connect the two remaining cables together, for example, using a typical electrical screw terminal.

Once this is done, you can connect the device you want to control the relay. Connect the lamp inside the female power socket, and then connect the male power plug to the power plug in the wall. The following image represents the system at this point, without the device to control being connected:

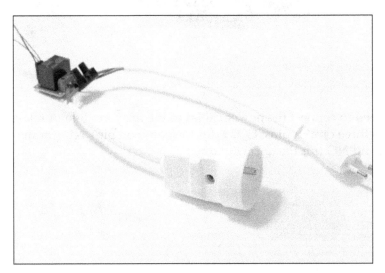

If you have something similar, congratulations! You are done with the hardware connections for this chapter.

Testing the relay

We are now going to build a very simple sketch to test the hardware connections we just made. The sketch will simply switch the relay on and off every second.

The sketch starts by declaring the right pin for the relay:

```
const int relay_pin = 7;
```

Then, we set this pin as an output:

```
pinMode(relay_pin,OUTPUT);
```

Then, in the loop() function of the sketch, we set the relay to a HIGH state:

```
digitalWrite(relay_pin, HIGH);
```

We wait for 5 seconds:

```
delay(5000)
```

Then, we switch the relay pin to a LOW state again:

```
digitalWrite(relay_pin, LOW);
```

We then wait again for 5 seconds:

```
delay(5000);
```

 The code for this section can be found in the GitHub repository for this chapter at https://github.com/openhomeautomation/arduino-networking/tree/master/chapter4.

You can now upload the code to the Arduino board. You should hear the relay switching on and off every second. If you connect a lamp to the project, for example, you should also see it switching on and off every second.

Controlling the relay remotely

Now, we are going to build our first interesting application using the system we just assembled. We are going to build an Arduino sketch to control the relay from anywhere within your local network. For example, if your computer is connected via Wi-Fi to your router and the Ethernet shield is connected to the same router, you will be able to control the relay via your computer. The advantage of this approach in this section is that even if your Internet connection is down, you will still be able to control the relay.

The application starts by including the correct libraries:

```
#include <SPI.h>
#include <Ethernet.h>
#include <aREST.h>
```

We set up the MAC address of the board:

```
byte mac[] = { 0x90, 0xA2, 0xDA, 0x0E, 0xFE, 0x40 };
```

We also define a default IP address for the board that will be used if DHCP fails:

```
IPAddress ip(192,168,1,150);
```

We then create an instance of the aREST library, which will handle the request that comes to the board:

```
aREST rest = aREST();
```

You also need to create an instance of the Ethernet server:

```
EthernetServer server(80);
```

In the setup() function of the sketch, we get an IP address using DHCP, as shown in the following code snippet:

```
if (Ethernet.begin(mac) == 0) {
  Serial.println("Failed to configure Ethernet using DHCP");
  Ethernet.begin(mac, ip);
}
```

Print the IP address on the Serial Monitor, using the following code:

```
server.begin();
Serial.print("Server is at ");
Serial.println(Ethernet.localIP());
```

Finally, in the `loop()` function of the sketch, we check whether there are incoming clients and handle these clients with the `aREST` instance:

```
EthernetClient client = server.available();
rest.handle(client);
```

 The code for this section can be found in the GitHub repository for this chapter at `https://github.com/openhomeautomation/ arduino-networking/tree/master/chapter4`.

You can now upload the code to the Arduino board and open the Serial Monitor. You should see the IP address of the board being printed out:

Server is at 192.168.1.103

You can now go to your web browser and start typing in commands. The `aREST` library allows you to directly command all the pins of the Arduino board via Ethernet. You can find the complete documentation of the library at `https:// github.com/marcoschwartz/aREST`. For example, we first need to set pin number 7 as an output. This is done using the following command:

http://192.168.1.103/mode/7/o

You will be greeted with the following message in the browser:

Pin D7 set to output

Now, to set the pin to a `HIGH` state, you can simply type:

http://192.168.1.103/digital/7/1

You will get the confirmation in your browser:

Pin D7 set to 1

You should also hear the relay switching from one state to the other when you enter the command.

Now we are going to build the server-side interface to control the relay from your computer without having to enter commands manually in your browser.

The interface is based on HTML, JavaScript, and PHP. In the HTML file, there are basically two buttons: one to turn the relay on and one to turn the relay off. The following is the code for one of the buttons:

```
<button class="btn btn-block btn-lg btn-primary" type="button"
id="1" onClick="buttonClick(this.id)">On</button>
```

You can see that the button calls a function, which is defined in a JavaScript file. Now let's have a look at this file. The first thing we have to do when the page loads is set the relay pin to be an output, just as we did when we typed commands directly in the browser. This is done using the following piece of code:

```
window.onload = function() {
  $.get( "command.php", {command: "/mode/7/o"} );
}
```

You can see that we are calling a file named command.php. We will see the details of this file later. Now, we saw earlier that every time a button is clicked, it calls a function called buttonClick. The following function is also defined in the JavaScript file:

```
function buttonClick(clicked_id){
```

Depending on which button was clicked, we send the corresponding command to the Arduino board. For example, for the **On** button, we put a HIGH state on the relay pin, as shown in the following code:

```
if (clicked_id == "1"){
  $.get( "command.php", {command: "/digital/7/1"} );
}
```

Finally, we have to look at the PHP file that will actually send the command to the board. We first need to get the command that was sent by the JavaScript file and store it in a variable:

```
$command = $_GET['command'];
```

Then, we need to set the URL to which we will send the command. To send the command to the board, we will use a PHP module called cURL, which will do exactly the same as what we just did from the web browser.

At this point, you will have to modify the IP address defined in the PHP file and replace it with the IP address of your board. The following piece of code does just that:

```
$service_url = 'http://192.168.1.103' . $command;
$curl = curl_init($service_url);
```

Then, we can actually perform the cURL call using the following piece of code:

```
curl_setopt($curl, CURLOPT_IPRESOLVE, CURL_IPRESOLVE_V4 );
curl_setopt($curl, CURLOPT_CONNECTTIMEOUT, 0.5);
$curl_response = curl_exec($curl);
curl_close($curl);
```

 The code for this section can be found in the GitHub repository for this chapter at https://github.com/openhomeautomation/arduino-networking/tree/master/chapter4.

We can now test the interface. Make sure that all the files of this interface are stored inside a folder at the root of your web server folder, and also make sure that the web server is running. Then, go to this folder via the localhost path in your browser and open the HTML file. You should see the following screenshot:

Try to click on one of the buttons: you should hear that the relay instantly switches according to the button you clicked.

 When you loaded the interface in your browser, the relay pin was also automatically set to be an output.

Controlling the relay from anywhere

In the last section of this chapter, we are going to take another approach. So far, we have a server running on our Arduino board, which can receive commands from any device on your local network. However, this is not convenient if you want to control a device from anywhere in the world. For example, you want to activate a lamp in your home at given intervals when you are away from your home.

To do so, we are going to use the Teleduino service, which allows you to do exactly that. The Arduino Ethernet shield will be constantly connected to this service, so you can transmit commands to the board from anywhere in the world if you have an Internet connection. We are going to build a new sketch for the Arduino board and then adapt the interface accordingly, so you can control the relay from anywhere in the world right from your web browser.

You first need to include the required libraries:

```
#include <EEPROM.h>
#include <Servo.h>
#include <Wire.h>
#include <Teleduino328.h>
#include <SPI.h>
#include <Ethernet.h>
```

Then you need to define the MAC address of your Ethernet shield:

```
byte mac[] = { 0x90, 0xA2, 0xDA, 0x0E, 0xFE, 0x40 };
```

Then, define a lot of parameters for the Teleduino service. As we will use DHCP to get an IP address, you don't need to change anything in the following code:

```
IPAddress deviceIp(192, 168, 1, 100); // Only if useDhcp is false
IPAddress gatewayIp(192, 168, 1, 1); // Only if useDhcp is false
IPAddress dnsIp(192, 168, 1, 1); // Only if useDhcp is false
IPAddress subnet(255, 255, 255, 0); // Only if useDhcp is false
IPAddress serverIp(173, 230, 152, 173); // Only if useDns is false
char serverName[] = "us01.proxy.teleduino.org"; // Only if useDns
is true
unsigned int serverPort = 5353; // Can be set to either 53 or 5353
byte statusLedPin = 8;
```

We also need to enter the key that you got at the beginning of the chapter. However, you will need to convert this key to the correct format so that you can insert it inside the Arduino sketch.

You can do so by visiting the following URL:

```
https://www.teleduino.org/tools/arduino-sketch-key
```

You will be prompted to insert the key inside the new window, as shown in the following screenshot:

You can then copy and paste the result inside the Arduino sketch:

```
byte key[] = { 0x64, 0x26, 0xFF, 0xC9,
               0x20, 0x4D, 0xF1, 0xCF,
               0xAE, 0x42, 0xD4, 0x1A,
               0xED, 0x6C, 0xB0, 0xB7 };
```

You also need to define the following variables so that the Teleduino service can work:

```
byte data[257];
byte dataLength;
byte hexStage;
unsigned long lastInstruction = 0;
unsigned long lastRefresh = 0;
byte stage = 0;
```

Finally, define an Ethernet client:

```
EthernetClient Client;
```

The rest of the sketch comes from the Teleduino example and won't be detailed here.

 The code for this section can be found in the GitHub repository for this chapter at https://github.com/openhomeautomation/arduino-networking/tree/master/chapter4.

It's now time to make a first test of this sketch. Upload the sketch to your Arduino board, and then go to your web browser. You can now directly send commands to your board. First, we are going to set the relay pin as an output as seen earlier. This is done using the following command (where you have to insert your own key at the k parameter):

```
http://us01.proxy.teleduino.org/api/1.0/328.php?k=yourKey
&r=definePinMode&pin=7&mode=1
```

You will be greeted by a confirmation message inside your web browser. You can now switch the relay pin to a HIGH state using the following command:

```
http://us01.proxy.teleduino.org/api/1.0/328.php?k=yourKey&r=setDigitalOut
put&pin=7&output=1
```

By doing so, you should hear the click of the relay, meaning the command was correctly sent. You will also be greeted by a confirmation message inside your browser.

Now, we are going to modify the interface so you can command the relay from anywhere using your web browser. Inside the JavaScript file, you will then need to define your Teleduino API key:

```
var key = "yourAPIkey";
```

Then, we have to change the command parameters to fit the Teleduino API and mention the key as well, as shown in the following code:

```
window.onload = function() {
  $.get( "command.php", {
  key: key, command: "definePinMode&pin=7&mode=1"} );
}
```

Also, we have to change the command parameters and mention the key for the function that is called when a button is clicked:

```
if (clicked_id == "1"){
  $.get( "command.php", {
  key: key, command: "setDigitalOutput&pin=7&output=1"} );
}
```

Inside the PHP file, we now have to get two parameters, the command and API key from Teleduino:

```
$key = $_GET['key'];
$command = $_GET['command'];
```

We also need to modify the service URL, as shown in the following code:

```
$service_url =
'http://us01.proxy.teleduino.org/api/1.0/328.php?k=' .
$key . '&r=' . $command;
$curl = curl_init($service_url);
```

The rest of the files are strictly identical, as seen in the previous section.

> The code for this section can be found in the GitHub repository for this chapter at https://github.com/openhomeautomation/ arduino-networking/tree/master/chapter4.

You can now put all the files for this modified interface inside a folder at the root of your web server. Also, make sure that the web server is still running. You can open the HTML file and you should see exactly the same interface as before.

You can now try to click on a button and you should instantly hear the relay switch. The advantage over the previous section of the chapter is that this interface can now work from anywhere. You can be in one part of the world and have your Ethernet shield in another part of the world and it would still work.

Summary

In this chapter, we interfaced a relay to the Arduino board and the Ethernet shield so that it can be controlled remotely. To do so, we used two different approaches, each with their own advantages and disadvantages. First, we kept things local and controlled the relay from within your local network. This solution has the advantage that even if your Internet connection is down, the project still works.

Then, we used a dedicated web service to control the relay from anywhere. This is clearly an advantage of the latter approach; however, it will not work if your Ethernet shield is not connected to the web.

The following were the major takeaways from this chapter:

- First, we chose the different components for the project, and assembled them so that we can control a device from the Arduino board such as a desk lamp.
- Then, we wrote the first sketch to test the project by simply switching the relay on and off.

- After that, we built the first application based on the hardware we just assembled. We used a dedicated library so that the Arduino board could receive commands from the network using the Ethernet shield. We also built a simple web-based interface so that you can control the relay from a graphical interface running on your computer.

- Finally, we used a web service called Teleduino to control the relay from anywhere in the world. We also modified the graphical interface so that we can control the relay from anywhere.

In the next chapter, we are going to take yet another approach and use the Ethernet shield to connect our Arduino projects to the **Internet of Things**. We are going to perform some measurements on the Arduino board and send this data right to a cloud service. Using this service, we will be able to monitor the measurements that come from the board in real time and from anywhere in the world.

5
Internet of Things with Xively

In the previous chapters of the book, we mainly kept things local when performing measurements on the Arduino board with the Ethernet shield. For example, we sent some measured data back to a database on your computer and displayed the measurements there.

In this chapter, we are going to take a different approach. We are going to integrate the Ethernet shield into an **Internet of Things** perspective. This means that instead of logging measurements locally within your local network, we are going to automatically send the measured data to a cloud service called **Xively**. The purpose of the Xively website is to store data that comes from your devices and display this data on their website. This way, your data will be available at any time and can be accessed from anywhere.

The following will be the major takeaways from this chapter:

- First, we are going to build the hardware for this project around the Ethernet shield and the DHT11 temperature and humidity sensor.

- Then, we will create an account on the Xively website. We will also configure this account so that we can send the measured data to it using the Arduino Ethernet shield.

- When the account is correctly set, we will use the account information such as the Xively API key to build the Arduino sketch for this project.

- Finally, we will upload the sketch to the Arduino board and test it. We will check that the data is correctly sent to the Arduino board and visualize the recorded data in real time in your browser.

Hardware and software requirements

On the hardware side, you will of course need the Arduino Ethernet shield and an Arduino board such as the Arduino Uno.

You will also need a sensor to measure some data. As this book is about how to use the Ethernet shield and not how to measure from sensors, you can actually use a sensor of your choice.

I picked a DHT11 sensor, which is a digital temperature and humidity sensor. I chose this sensor as it is a very cheap sensor and easy to interface with Arduino. Along with the DHT11 sensor, you will also need a 4.7k ohm resistor.

You will also need a breadboard and some jumper wires to make the connections between the sensor and the Ethernet shield.

On the software side, the first thing you will need is the library to interface with the sensor you chose before. As I chose a DHT11 sensor for this project, you will need to download and install the DHT library from `https://github.com/adafruit/DHT-sensor-library`.

To install an Arduino library, simply unzip the contents of the downloaded file into your `libraries` folder of your main Arduino folder (or create this folder if it doesn't exist already).

Hardware configuration

It's now time to set up the hardware for this project. At this point, if you followed one of the previous chapters, you should already have your Arduino Ethernet shield plugged into the Arduino board, one Ethernet cable connecting the Ethernet shield, and your Internet router. If that's not the case already, please do so.

The only thing you will have to connect in this project is the DHT11 sensor and the resistor. You can have an overview of the different connections you have to make by looking at the following schematic diagram:

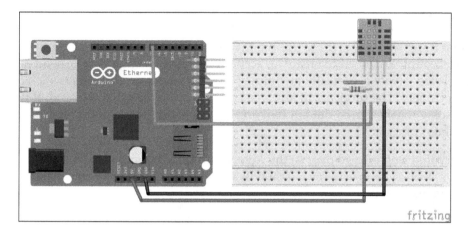

First, plug the DHT11 sensor to the breadboard. Then, connect pin numbers 1 and 2 of the sensor using the 4.7k ohm resistor.

Now comes the power supply. Connect the pin number 1 of the sensor to the Arduino 5 V and the pin number 4 to the Arduino GND. Finally, connect the pin number 2 of the DHT sensor to the Arduino pin number 7.

At the end, it should look like the following image:

You are now done with the hardware configuration of this project and can move to the next step, which is creating an account on Xively.

Creating your Xively account

The first thing we have to do to use the Xively service is create and configure a Xively account. You need to create an account on Xively so that we can send data to their service. Xively is basically an online platform for connected objects such as our Ethernet shield. The service will automatically store the data that we send. It will also display the measured data in the form of graphs that are updated in real time as the data comes in.

The very first step is to go over to the Xively signup page on their website at `https://xively.com/signup/`. You will arrive at a page where you can enter your personal details:

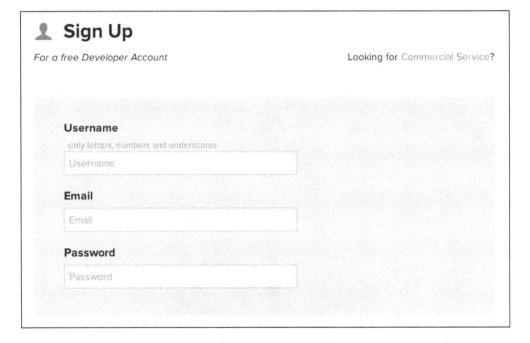

Then, you will need to create a device, which is a virtual entity on the Xively website. This device will receive the measured data. When you create a new device, you will need to enter a name for your device:

Then, you can add channels to your device. A channel on Xively is like a variable or a row in a database; it is the entity that will receive a specific measurement from the Arduino board. You can create a new channel on the page of your device by clicking on the button shown in the following screenshot:

You will need to enter some name for your channels. You will have to create two of them for this project: one called `Temperature` and one called `Humidity`.

Then, you will need to get some information about your account, which are all located on the device page.

The first one is the feed ID, which identifies this specific device. You can find it in the following section of the page:

Then, you will have to get your API key, which is specific to your account. You can also find it on the device page, as shown in the following screenshot:

You will need to enter these two keys inside the Arduino sketch that we will build in this chapter, so keep them at hand.

Sending data to Xively

We are now going to build the Arduino sketch for this project. The goal is to measure data on the Arduino board, connect with the Xively server, and send the data.

The first step is to include the following required libraries:

```
#include <SPI.h>
#include <Ethernet.h>
#include "DHT.h"
```

Enter the MAC address of your board:

```
byte mac[] = { 0x90, 0xA2, 0xDA, 0x0E, 0xFE, 0x40 };
```

We can then define the pin and the type of the DHT sensor as follows:

```
#define DHTPIN 7
#define DHTTYPE DHT11
```

Create an instance on the sensor, as shown in the following line:

```
DHT dht(DHTPIN, DHTTYPE);
```

Create an instance of the Ethernet client:

```
EthernetClient client;
```

We also define a default IP address for the board:

```
IPAddress ip(192,168,1,50);
```

In the sketch, we also set the address of the secured Xively server that we will connect to using the Ethernet shield:

```
IPAddress server(216,52,233,120);
```

Now, we have to modify the sketch a little bit to enter your own information about your Xively account. This is where you have to enter your API key and feed ID that you got in the previous section. Using the following code, you can define your API key and feed ID:

```
#define WEBSITE  "api.xively.com"
#define API_key  "yourAPIKey"
#define feedID   "yourFeedID"
```

In the setup() function of the sketch, we can now use DHCP to get an IP address for the sketch, as shown in the following code:

```
// Start the Ethernet connection
if (Ethernet.begin(mac) == 0) {
  Serial.println("Failed to configure Ethernet using DHCP");
  Ethernet.begin(mac, ip);
}
```

For debug purposes, we print this IP address on the Serial Monitor:

```
Serial.print("IP address: ");
Serial.println(Ethernet.localIP());
```

Now, in the loop() function of the sketch, we will make the measurements with the DHT sensor, format the data for Xively, and send this data to the Xively server.

The first step is to make the measurements. This is done with the following lines of code:

```
float humidity = dht.readHumidity();
float temperature = dht.readTemperature();
```

We then need to format this measured data so the Xively server can understand it. Indeed, Xively defines a specific format to receive data. All the formats are defined at https://xively.com/dev/docs/api/communicating/data_formats/.

In our case, we will need to put the data in a JSON string according to the Xively specifications. This is done using the following piece of code:

```
int length = 0;
String data = "";
data = data + "\n" + "{\"version\":\"1.0.0\",\"datastreams\" : [
{\"id\" : \"Temperature\",\"current_value\" : \"" + String((int)
temperature) + "\"}," + "{\"id\" : \"Humidity\",\"current_value\" :
\"" + String((int)humidity) + "\"}]}";
Serial.println(data);
length = data.length();
```

You will note that we also get the length of the string that we will also need in order to send the data to the Xively server. Also, we are using backslashes before quotations marks to indicate that we want to transmit quotation marks and not the end of the string.

Then, we will actually connect to the Xively server and send the data. This is done by using a PUT request and sending a JSON file to the Xively server. In the header of the request, we define the feed ID of the Xively device and we also transmit your Xively API key.

We also need to send the data we defined before in the body of the request. This is done using the following piece of code:

```
if (client.connect(server, 80)) {
  if (client.connected()) {
    Serial.println("connected");
    client.println("PUT /v2/feeds/" + String(feedID) + ".json
    HTTP/1.1");
    client.println("Host: api.xively.com");
    client.println("X-ApiKey: " + String(API_key));
    client.println("Content-Length: " + String(length));
    client.print("Connection: close");
    client.println();
    client.print(data);
    client.println();
  } else {
    Serial.println(F("Connection failed"));
    return;
  }
}
```

Then, after the data is sent, we read back the data coming from the server and print the answer on the Serial Monitor for debugging purposes, using the following piece of code:

```
while (client.connected()) {
  while (client.available()) {
    char c = client.read();
    Serial.print(c);
  }
}
```

Finally, when it is over, we stop the connection. This is done with the following code:

```
if (!client.connected()) {
  Serial.println();
  Serial.println("disconnecting.");
  client.stop();
}
```

We repeat the entire process every 10 seconds with the following line:

```
delay(10000);
```

 All the code for this chapter can be found on the GitHub repository of this chapter at https://github.com/openhomeautomation/ arduino-networking/tree/master/chapter5.

It is now time to test the sketch and upload data to Xively. You can upload the sketch to Xively at this point, and open the Serial Monitor in the Arduino IDE. You should see that the IP address of the board is being printed out, and that the sketch is connected to the Xively server:

```
IP address: 192.168.1.104

Connecting...
```

You should also see how the data was formatted for Xively:

```
{"version":"1.0.0","datastreams" : [ {"id" : "Temperature","current_
value" : "24"},{"id" : "Humidity","current_value" : "37"}]}
```

After a moment, you should see the answer coming back from Xively. If the data was sent correctly to the Xively server, you should see a 200 OK code being printed out to the Serial Monitor:

```
HTTP/1.1 200 OK

Date: Wed, 21 May 2014 15:02:49 GMT
```

```
Content-Type: application/json; charset=utf-8

Content-Length: 0

Connection: close

X-Request-Id: e44becaa5231354568262013fa713d9f099ffc83

Cache-Control: max-age=0

Vary: Accept-Encoding
```

This means that the data was correctly received by the Xively server, and in an understandable format.

If that is not the case, there are several things you can check. First, make sure that the Internet connection of your Ethernet shield is working, and that the shield is indeed receiving an IP address. Then, make sure that you correctly entered your Xively information, meaning the API key and the feed ID. Also, check that you correctly formatted your data in the JSON format, which we introduced while writing the sketch. Finally, make sure that the DHT sensor is correctly wired and measuring data properly, as it could interfere with the normal behavior of the rest of the sketch.

Visualizing the recorded data

We are now going to visualize the data we recorded with Xively. You can go over again to the device page on the Xively website. You should see that some data has been recorded in different channels, as shown in the following screenshot:

By clicking on one of these channels, you can also display the data graphically. For example, the following screenshot shows the temperature channel after a few measurements:

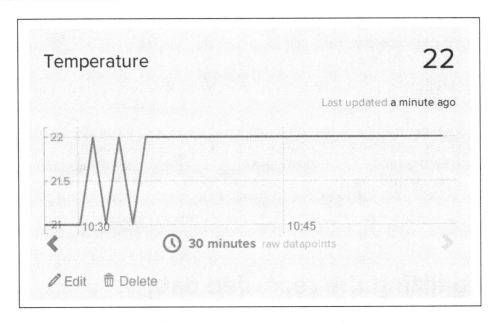

After a while, you will have more points for the temperature measurements, as shown in the following screenshot:

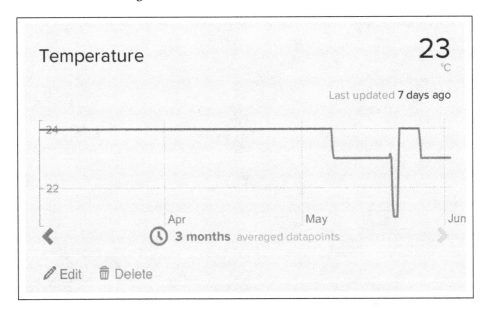

You can also do the same for the humidity measurements; the following screenshot shows the humidity measurements:

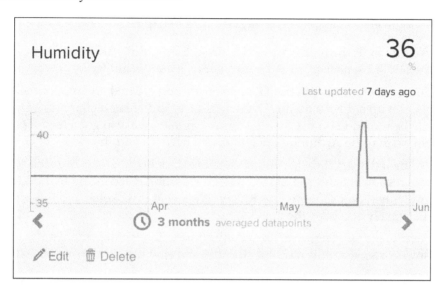

Note that by clicking on the time icon, you can change the time axis and display a longer or shorter time range.

If you don't see any data being displayed, you need to go back to the Arduino IDE and make sure that the answer coming from the Xively server is a 200 OK message, like we saw in the previous section.

Summary

Let's summarize what we did in this chapter. We used the Ethernet shield to build an Internet of Things project, as we connected the Ethernet shield directly to a cloud service. We measured data on the Arduino board and sent this data to the cloud service Xively so that it can be accessed and displayed from anywhere.

The advantage of this solution is that the data recorded on Xively is accessible from anywhere, and not only from your local network. You can also use the data and Xively to create automated triggers based on the data. You can, for example, send a request to another website based on the recorded data. You can also share the data that is recorded by your device with colleagues or friends so that they can also monitor what your project is recording in real time.

Of course, one of the drawbacks from this solution is that if your Internet connection is down, the whole project won't work at all.

The following were the major takeaways from this chapter:

- We first built the hardware of this project, including the Ethernet shield and the DHT11 sensor to measure temperature and humidity.

- Then, we went over to the Xively website and created an account there. We also set up a device on the Xively interface, and created channels so that data can be recorded on the Xively website. Finally, we also got a feed ID and API key so that the Arduino sketch knows where to send the data.

- We then designed the Arduino sketch for this project. The Arduino sketch was responsible for measuring data, formatting it according to the Xively guidelines, and sending it to Xively. We tested this sketch and made sure that Xively accepted the data.

- Finally, we went again to the Xively website to visualize the data. We learned how to visualize this data graphically, and saw the data arrive in real time.

In the next chapter, we are going to continue building Internet of Things applications. We are going to use another web service called **Temboo**, which is a platform that can be interfaced with other services such as Gmail or Google Docs. We are going to use this service to record data directly on a Google Docs spreadsheet and send automated e-mails based on the recorded data.

6
Logging Data in Google Docs

In this chapter, we are going to continue building Internet of Things applications using the Arduino Ethernet shield. This time, we are going to use the web service Temboo, to build some useful and interesting applications. Temboo is different from Xively, which we used in the previous chapter. It is not a cloud platform in itself, but it can be used to interface our Arduino projects with several other applications and services. You can see Temboo as a bridge between your Ethernet shield and a wide range of web services, such as e-mail services, text messaging services, or storage services.

For example, in this chapter, we are going see how to interface your Arduino project to your Google Account via Temboo. We will use this functionality to automatically log measurements inside a Google Docs spreadsheet.

The advantage of this solution is that you can access your Google Docs spreadsheet from anywhere, thus monitoring your data from anywhere in the world while your Ethernet shield is sending data from home. We are also going to send automated e-mail alerts using Gmail based on the measured data.

The following will be the major takeaways of this chapter:

- First, we are going to configure the hardware part of this project using the Ethernet shield and the DHT11 sensor. We are also going to download and install the required libraries for the project, including the Temboo Arduino library.
- Then, we will set up the different accounts that we need for this chapter. First, we will set up your Google Account and create a spreadsheet where the data will be logged. We are also going to set up a Temboo account and configure it to use the Arduino Ethernet shield.

- Once all the accounts are set, we are going to build the first application of this project—automatic log measured data in a Google Docs spreadsheet. You will be able to see the measured data recorded live in the spreadsheet and the data being plotted automatically in real time.

- Finally, we are going to set up our Arduino system to automatically send e-mails when a given measurement exceeds a threshold.

Hardware and software requirements

On the hardware side, you will of course need the Arduino Ethernet shield and an Arduino board such as the Arduino Uno.

You will also need a sensor to measure some data. As this book is about how to use the Ethernet shield and not how to measure from sensors, you could actually take any sensor of your choice.

I used a DHT11 sensor, which is a digital temperature and humidity sensor. I chose this sensor for this chapter and for many chapters of the book as it is a very cheap sensor and it is easy to interface with Arduino. Along with the DHT11 sensor, you will also need a 4.7k ohm resistor.

You will also need a breadboard and some jumper wires to create the connections between the sensor and the Ethernet shield.

On the software side, the first thing you will need is the library to interface with the sensor you chose before. As I chose a DHT11 sensor for this project, you will need to download and install the DHT library from `https://github.com/adafruit/DHT-sensor-library` in order to use this.

You will also need to download and install the Arduino Temboo library from `https://www.temboo.com/arduino/others/library-installation`.

To install an Arduino library, simply unzip the contents of the downloaded file to your `libraries` folder of your main Arduino folder (or create this folder if it doesn't exist already).

Hardware configuration

It's now time to set up the hardware for this project. At this point, if you followed one of the previous chapters, you should already have your Arduino Ethernet shield plugged to the Arduino board, one Ethernet cable connecting the Ethernet shield, and your Internet router. If that's not the case already, please do so.

The only thing you will have to connect in this project is the DHT11 sensor and the resistor. You can have an overview of the different connections you have to make by looking at the following schematic diagram:

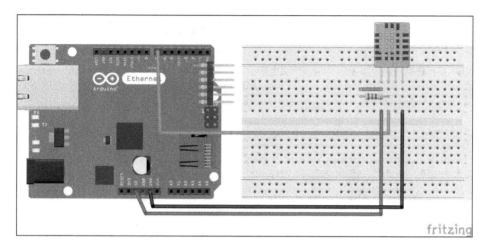

First, plug the DHT11 sensor to the breadboard. Then, connect pin number 1 and 2 of the sensor using the 4.7k ohm resistor.

Now, we are going to connect the power supply. Connect pin number 1 of the sensor to the Arduino 5V, and pin number 4 to the Arduino GND. Finally, connect pin number 2 of the DHT sensor to the Arduino pin number 7.

At the end, the connections should look like the following screenshot:

You are now done with the hardware configuration of this project and you can move to the next step, that is, setting up your Google Account for this project.

Setting up your Google Account

For this project, you will need to have a Google Account. If you are already using a service such as Gmail or YouTube, it means you already have a Google Account, and you will be able to use Google Docs immediately. If this is not the case, you can create an account at the following address:

```
https://docs.google.com
```

Once your account is created, you will be able to create your first spreadsheet. To do so, just click on the **Create** button and select **Spreadsheet**. You will have to enter a name for the spreadsheet, which is important as you will need to provide this name to Temboo later. I named my sheet simply `Ethernet`.

Then, you will need to give names to the columns that will receive the data. We are going to measure temperature and humidity and also add a timestamp to each measurement. You will need to enter this in the first row, as shown in the following screenshot:

	A	B	C
1	Timestamp	Temperature	Humidity
2			
3			
4			

When you have a Google spreadsheet that looks like this, it means that you are all set up for this part and that you can move to the next part.

Creating your Temboo account

The next step is to create an account on Temboo. To do this, simply go to the following address:

```
https://www.temboo.com/
```

You will be greeted with a page that asks you to enter your e-mail address.

Once your account is created, you will be taken to the Temboo main page. You will have many choices at this stage, but the one we are looking for is **Devices**, which is displayed in the following screenshot:

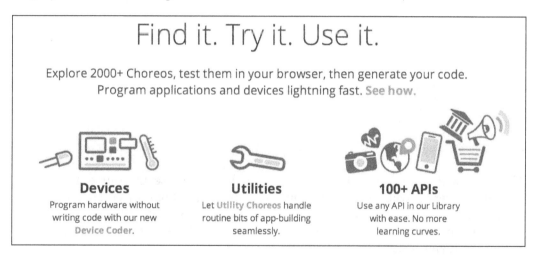

Inside the devices page, Temboo proposes a tool called **Device Coder**. This tool is intended to generate most of the code for us when we use a platform such as the Arduino Yun, or in our case, the Arduino Ethernet shield.

Simply click on the right choice, which corresponds to other Arduino devices such as the Ethernet shield, as shown in the following screenshot:

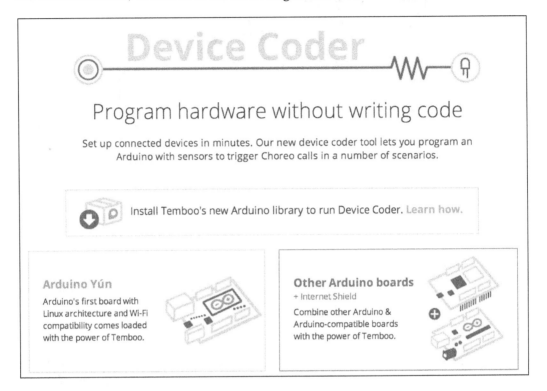

Then, you will be asked which kind of sensor you want to use. Of course, Temboo cannot list every possible sensor we could use for this kind of project. Therefore, the DHT11 sensor is not in the list of possible devices. However, we will fix this by rewriting part of the generated code. For now, simply choose **Generic sensor**. Then in the next menu, select **Spreadsheet**.

You will then be taken to a new menu where you can configure your device. As this is your first time configuring the device, you will be asked to create new Temboo credentials for your Ethernet shield. A Temboo credential is a set of parameters that are stored on the Temboo servers so that you don't have to enter them later while developing your applications.

Enter the details about your Arduino board and Ethernet shield in the credentials box, as shown in the following screenshot:

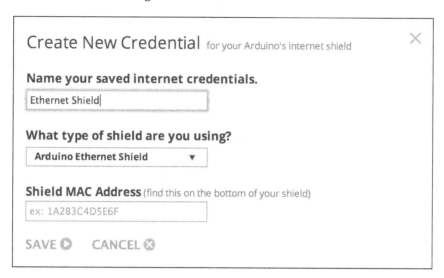

Then, just as you selected to work with a spreadsheet, you will also need to enter your Google Account credentials. We will use it to access Google Docs and also in the final part of the chapter to interface with Gmail.

Enter all your Google Account information in the box, which is shown in the following screenshot:

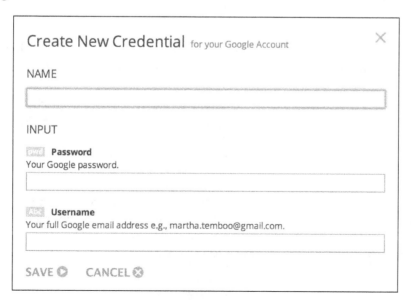

For the name of my Google Account credential, I used `EthernetGmail`.

Note that if you have the Google 2-Step authentication method activated, you will need to provide an application-specific password here. This is done for security reasons, so your Google Account doesn't get compromised if Temboo gets compromised. You can find more information about application-specific passwords at `https://support.google.com/accounts/answer/185833?hl=en`.

You can also choose not to enter your Google information at this point. However, in that case, you will need to enter it inside the Arduino sketch and modify this sketch slightly. To find more information about this, you can visit `https://www.temboo.com/arduino/yun/update-google-spreadsheet`.

You will also be asked to give a name of a spreadsheet you prepared before. Simply enter this name in the correct box, as shown in the following screenshot:

And the name of your spreadsheet?

mySpreadsheet

For example, I named my spreadsheet `Ethernet`:

And the name of your spreadsheet?

Ethernet

After that, you will have to select the device you will be working with to log data to the spreadsheet. This is where you select the credentials that we created before, as shown in the following screenshot:

How does your board connect to the internet?

EthernetShield ▼

You will also need to give a name to the project you just created so your Arduino sketch will later on know where to send the data. I named mine `arduinoTemperatureSpreadsheet`. If you decide to use another name, you will have to make a small modification in the code later.

When this is done, you will be prompted to download a compressed file that contains two Arduino code files. Download it, unzip it, and have a look at it. It will appear like the following screenshot:

There should be an Arduino file and another file called TembooAccount.h. This last file is the most important as it contains your credentials for the project. You will need to use this file for the rest of the project in place of the file that is included in the GitHub repository of the project.

Logging data in a spreadsheet

After finishing the configuration of our device on the Temboo website, we downloaded a bunch of files from Temboo. However, the Arduino file that was downloaded is for a generic sensor. In this section, we are going to adapt this file for our own needs and see the details of how the code works.

You will need to insert your own TembooAccount.h file in the same folder as the Arduino file so that the code can work.

The main Arduino sketch for this section starts by including all the libraries that are required for the project to work with Temboo. Note that we will also insert the DHT library. Add the following libraries in the code:

```
#include <SPI.h>
#include <Dhcp.h>
#include <Dns.h>
#include <Ethernet.h>
#include <EthernetClient.h>
#include <Temboo.h>
#include "TembooAccount.h"
#include "DHT.h"
```

We also define the pin on which the DHT sensor is connected and the type of the sensor:

```
#define DHTPIN 7
#define DHTTYPEDHT11
```

Then, we will create an instance of the sensor:

```
DHTdht(DHTPIN, DHTTYPE);
```

We also assign the MAC address of the Ethernet shield. Note that here it is not explicitly assigned, but the information is directly taken from your Temboo account file. The MAC address is assigned with the following line:

```
byte ethernetMACAddress[] = ETHERNET_SHIELD_MAC;
```

We will also create an instance of an Ethernet client as follows:

```
EthernetClient client;
```

Now, in the `setup()` function of the sketch, we will get an IP address for the Ethernet shield via DHCP, as shown in the following code:

```
Serial.print("DHCP:");
if (Ethernet.begin(ethernetMACAddress) == 0) {
  Serial.println("FAIL");
  while(true);
}
Serial.println("OK");
delay(5000);
```

Start the DHT sensor with the following line:

```
dht.begin();
```

Then, in the `loop()` function, we will measure the temperature and humidity from the DHT sensor and convert the measurements to strings with the following piece of code:

```
float h = dht.readHumidity();
float t = dht.readTemperature();

int temperature = (int)t;
int humidity = (int)h;

Serial.println("Temperature: " + String(temperature));
Serial.println("Humidity: " + String(humidity));
```

After the measurements are done, we will call the following function that will actually connect to the web and log the data to our Google Docs spreadsheet. We are going to see the details of this function that was autogenerated by Temboo in a moment:

```
runAppendRow(temperature, humidity);
```

Finally, we will also insert some delay between each measurement. I recommend using a large delay (I chose to log data every minute for demonstration purposes) because the number of calls you can make to Temboo is limited. The delay is inserted with the following line:

```
delay(60000);
```

You can see the different plans and pricing at the following link:

```
https://www.temboo.com/about/plans
```

For example, on the free plan, you are limited to 1,000 calls per month, which means that you can log measurements approximately every 44 minutes. On the first paid plan, you can log one data point approximately every 5 minutes. Keep these limitations in mind while developing your applications.

Let's now see the details of the `runAppendRow()` function. It starts by declaring the type of Choreo we want to use. A Choreo is the equivalent of a library on the Temboo service. For example, we will declare that we want to use the specific library to insert data in a row in the Google Docs spreadsheet:

```
TembooChoreoAppendRowChoreo(client);
```

We will set the different information about your account, such as the name of the account and your app key. All these are already defined in your Temboo account file that you downloaded before, so you don't need to define anything more:

```
AppendRowChoreo.setAccountName(TEMBOO_ACCOUNT);
AppendRowChoreo.setAppKeyName(TEMBOO_APP_KEY_NAME);
AppendRowChoreo.setAppKey(TEMBOO_APP_KEY);
```

Then, you need to somehow specify where the data should be logged. Once more, all the work is done by Temboo: all the information is saved on the Temboo side in the Google Account credentials you have set before. If you used the same name as I did for this example, you don't have to modify anything in the following line:

```
AppendRowChoreo.setSavedInputs("arduinoTemperatureSpreadsheet");
```

Note that the new way to overcome the Temboo call limitation is also to transmit several data points at each call of the Temboo API, for example, by appending several rows at each call. You can modify the code accordingly as an exercise.

Now, we need to format the data so it can be recorded correctly in Google Docs. What you want to insert in a given row is a timestamp, the temperature, and the humidity. For the timestamp, we are simply going to use the time that has passed since the device was powered on with the `millis()` function.

The data itself will be contained inside a string variable, where the value of each column will be separated with a comma, as shown in the following code:

```
String RowDataValue = String(millis()) + "," + String(temperature)
+ "," + String(humidity);
AppendRowChoreo.addInput("RowData", RowDataValue);
```

We also need to set which Choreo we want to use with the following line:

```
AppendRowChoreo.setChoreo
("/Library/Google/Spreadsheets/AppendRow");
```

Then, we can finally execute Choreo and store the result in a variable called `returnCode` using the following line:

```
unsigned int returnCode = AppendRowChoreo.run();
```

If this code is equal to 0 after Choreo has been executed, it means that everything went fine, and we will print the corresponding message on the Serial Monitor for debugging purposes using the following piece of code:

```
if (returnCode == 0) {
  Serial.println("Done!\n");
} else {
  // A non-zero return code means there was an error
  // Read and print the error message
  while (AppendRowChoreo.available()) {
    char c = AppendRowChoreo.read();
    Serial.print(c);
  }
  Serial.println();
}
```

If that's not the case, we will print the corresponding error message on the Serial Monitor. Finally, we close Choreo with the following line:

```
AppendRowChoreo.close();
```

 You can find all the code for this section on the GitHub repository of this chapter at https://github.com/openhomeautomation/arduino-networking/tree/master/chapter6.

Even if you decide to get the code directly from the GitHub repository, note that you will need to take your own Temboo account file or enter the correct information in the Temboo account file provided on GitHub.

We can now test the project. Upload the code to the Arduino board, go to Google Docs, and open the spreadsheet of the project. After a moment, you should see the first measurements being logged inside the spreadsheet, as shown in the following screenshot:

	A	B	C
1	**Timestamp**	**Temperature**	**Humidity**
2	10122	23	35
3	28654	23	35

You can also use the integrated plotting functionalities of Google Docs to display the measurements on a graph. You can simply select the columns corresponding to the data (A, B, and C in the example developed in this chapter), and click on the **Insert Chart** button inside the toolbar. You will be prompted to choose the type of graph you want to plot. I simply chose a line chart to plot all the data on a single graph. The graph will look similar to the following screenshot:

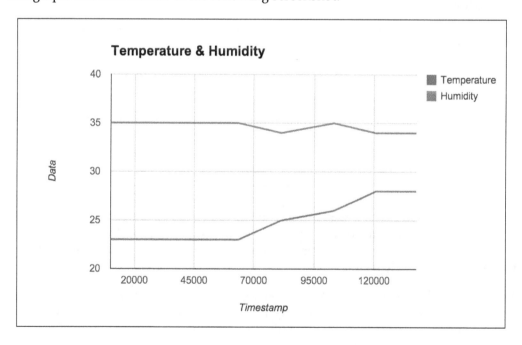

As everything is dynamic, you should see that the graph is updated in real time as new measurements come in. Note that as this is a spreadsheet on Google Docs, it is accessible from anywhere you are in the world, you just need to log in to your Google Account.

Sending automated e-mails

In this last part of the chapter, we are going to build on what we already did, but change the application slightly. This time, we are going to use the Ethernet shield and Temboo to automatically send e-mails when a condition is reached. As an example, we will set a condition on the measured temperature. Whenever the temperature reaches a given value, we will send an e-mail to the address of your choice, for example, your professional e-mail to keep you updated when you are at work.

It starts by going again to the Device Coder on the Temboo website at `https://www.temboo.com/library/Library/Devices/Arduino/Others/`.

Click on **Generic sensor** and then on **Email**. This time you won't have to enter that much information. Your Gmail account should already be set from the previous section and the Device Coder should automatically select your Ethernet shield.

You simply need to enter the destination e-mail (for example, your professional e-mail address or the e-mail address from a family member) and the **Subject** field of the e-mail. Do not worry now about the value of the body of the e-mail; we will change it later:

And what should the email say?	
TO	a@b.com, x@y.com
SUBJECT	Temperature change detected
BODY	The current sensor value is: {sensorValue}

When it is finished, click on **Generate**. As for the previous section, you will be prompted to enter a name for this project so that Temboo knows where to send e-mails. I named mine `arduinoTemperatureEmail`, but if you decide to use another name, you will simply have to change one line in the code later.

You can now download the generated code, which we will modify a bit. As for the previous section, we are going to modify the Arduino code, but it is important that you get your own `TembooAcccount.h` file that contains the information relative to your own account on Temboo.

The Arduino sketch is similar to the one in the previous section, so I will only discuss the main changes.

In the `loop()` function of the sketch, you need to set the limit at which the e-mail will be sent by Temboo. For demonstration purposes, I will set the limit to 23, as shown in the following code:

```
if (temperature > 23) {
    Serial.println("\nTriggered! Calling
    /Library/Google/Gmail/SendEmail...");

    // Send email
    runSendEmail(temperature);
}
```

You can see that every time the temperature goes above that limit, an alert will be sent by Temboo via e-mail. We will see the details of this function in a moment. I also inserted a 1-minute delay between each measurement, so we don't continuously send e-mails if the threshold is crossed:

```
delay(60000);
```

Now let's look at the details of the `runSendEmail()` function. This function is responsible for creating the correct Choreo to send an e-mail, set the body of the e-mail, and send it via Temboo.

It starts by creating the correct Choreo to send an e-mail with the following line:

```
TembooChoreoSendEmailChoreo(client);
```

We also define the different information relative to your account that is defined in the Temboo account file you just downloaded from Temboo:

```
SendEmailChoreo.setAccountName(TEMBOO_ACCOUNT);
SendEmailChoreo.setAppKeyName(TEMBOO_APP_KEY_NAME);
SendEmailChoreo.setAppKey(TEMBOO_APP_KEY);
```

Then, this is where you need to enter the name of the e-mail project that you just created on Temboo. If you use the same name as I did, there is no need to modify anything in the following line:

```
SendEmailChoreo.setSavedInputs("arduinoTemperatureEmail");
```

We will now build the body of the e-mail, which will be stored in a string variable. We simply use a generic message where we attach the value of the measured temperature and store everything in a string. Finally, we will add the following lines as an input to the Choreo used to send e-mails:

```
String MessageBodyValue = String("Alert! The current sensor value is:
") + String(sensorValue);
SendEmailChoreo.addInput("MessageBody", MessageBodyValue);
```

Just before executing Choreo, we define that we want to use `SendEmailChoreo` from Gmail using the following line:

```
SendEmailChoreo.setChoreo("/Library/Google/Gmail/SendEmail");
```

We can finally execute Choreo and store the result in a variable:

```
unsigned intreturnCode = SendEmailChoreo.run();
```

As in the previous section, if the result is `0`, it means everything went fine. If this is not the case, we will print the error message on the `Serial` port for debugging using the following piece of code:

```
if (returnCode == 0) {
  Serial.println("Done!\n");
} else {
  // A non-zero return code means there was an error
  // Read and print the error message
  while (SendEmailChoreo.available()) {
    char c = SendEmailChoreo.read();
    Serial.print(c);
  }
  Serial.println();
}
```

Finally, we will close Choreo with the following line:

```
SendEmailChoreo.close();
```

> You can find all the code for this section on the GitHub repository of this chapter at `https://github.com/openhomeautomation/arduino-networking/tree/MASTER/chapter6`.

You can now test the sketch. The first thing to do is to make sure that you have your own Temboo account file in the same folder as the Arduino sketch. Then, upload the sketch to the Arduino board and open the Serial Monitor. The first thing you should see is the confirmation message that everything went ok:

DHCP: OK

Setup complete

Then, you should see the first measurements on the Serial Monitor:

Temperature: 21

Humidity: 39

Depending on the temperature value, you might need to pinch your sensor to trigger the e-mail alert. Remember, in the example of this chapter, we set a value of 23 degrees for the temperature. After a while, if the temperature reaches the threshold, you should see the following message:

```
Triggered! Calling /Library/Google/Gmail/SendEmail...
```

After a while, the following confirmation message should appear:

```
Done!
```

You can now close the Serial Monitor and go check the e-mail account that you set on Temboo. You should have received a message with the title you set on Temboo, and you will also receive the body that indicates the generic message you set in the sketch along with the measured temperature.

Summary

In this chapter, we created another Internet of Things project using the web service Temboo. Based on Temboo, we built two exciting applications. The first one was to automatically log measurements inside a Google Docs spreadsheet. Compared to the approach we took in the previous chapter, the advantage here is clearly that Google Docs is the widely used standard to create and share spreadsheets. You can access your data from anywhere just by using a web browser, and you can also plot the data and share it easily with your friends and family.

We also built an exciting application where we interfaced our project with Gmail via Temboo. We built an automated e-mail alert system based on the measured data.

Let's see what the major takeaways of this chapter were. First, we built the hardware of the project, with the DHT11 temperature and humidity sensor on top of the Arduino Ethernet shield.

Then, we set up the different accounts that were needed for the project. We first created a spreadsheet on Google Docs and configured it correctly so it can work with Temboo. Then, we also created a Temboo account and configured it so that your Ethernet shield can send data to Temboo and log measurements to Google Docs.

After the setting up phase, we built the first application of this project, which consisted of logging data directly to a Google Docs spreadsheet. We also displayed this data using the Google Docs plotting capabilities.

Finally, we used Temboo again to create an automated e-mail alert system by sending an e-mail automatically to the address of your choice when a measurement reached a given threshold.

As this is the end of this book, let's see what we learned about the Arduino Ethernet shield and what exciting applications we can create with it.

The first part of the book was all about running a web client on the Ethernet shield. We made a first test by just trying out the shield and seeing whether it could connect to the Internet and grab the contents of a page. Then, we built our first measurement system, where the Ethernet shield was connecting to a server running to your computer to log some data.

In the second part of the book, we gave more autonomy to the Arduino Ethernet shield by running a web server right on the Arduino board. We made the measurement project again, but this time by having a web server run on the board and logging data to a SD card inserted in the shield. We also connected a relay to the Arduino board and we controlled it via Ethernet.

Finally, we built two Internet of Things project using the platforms Xively and Temboo. In both these projects, we sent data to the Web using the Ethernet shield so that this data can be accessed and displayed graphically from anywhere in the world.

To conclude this book, I hope that all the information you found in the different chapters will give you the will to build even more exciting applications. The Arduino Ethernet shield is one of the best ways to build amazing connected applications with Arduino, and there is no limit to what you can do with the concepts you learned in this book.

Index

Thank you for buying
Arduino Networking

About Packt Publishing

Packt, pronounced 'packed', published its first book "*Mastering phpMyAdmin for Effective MySQL Management*" in April 2004 and subsequently continued to specialize in publishing highly focused books on specific technologies and solutions.

Our books and publications share the experiences of your fellow IT professionals in adapting and customizing today's systems, applications, and frameworks. Our solution based books give you the knowledge and power to customize the software and technologies you're using to get the job done. Packt books are more specific and less general than the IT books you have seen in the past. Our unique business model allows us to bring you more focused information, giving you more of what you need to know, and less of what you don't.

Packt is a modern, yet unique publishing company, which focuses on producing quality, cutting-edge books for communities of developers, administrators, and newbies alike. For more information, please visit our website: www.packtpub.com.

About Packt Open Source

In 2010, Packt launched two new brands, Packt Open Source and Packt Enterprise, in order to continue its focus on specialization. This book is part of the Packt Open Source brand, home to books published on software built around Open Source licenses, and offering information to anybody from advanced developers to budding web designers. The Open Source brand also runs Packt's Open Source Royalty Scheme, by which Packt gives a royalty to each Open Source project about whose software a book is sold.

Writing for Packt

We welcome all inquiries from people who are interested in authoring. Book proposals should be sent to author@packtpub.com. If your book idea is still at an early stage and you would like to discuss it first before writing a formal book proposal, contact us; one of our commissioning editors will get in touch with you.

We're not just looking for published authors; if you have strong technical skills but no writing experience, our experienced editors can help you develop a writing career, or simply get some additional reward for your expertise.

Arduino Robotic Projects

ISBN: 978-1-78398-982-9   Paperback: 240 pages

Build awesome and complex robots with the power of Arduino

1. Develop a series of exciting robots that can sail, go under water, and fly.

2. Simple, easy-to-understand instructions to program Arduino.

3. Effectively control the movements of all types of motors using Arduino.

C Programming for Arduino

ISBN: 978-1-84951-758-4   Paperback: 512 pages

Learn how to program and use Arduino boards with a series of engaging examples, illustrating each core concept

1. Use Arduino boards in your own electronic hardware and software projects.

2. Sense the world by using several sensory components with your Arduino boards.

3. Create tangible and reactive interfaces with your computer.

Internet of Things with the Arduino Yún

ISBN: 978-1-78328-800-7   Paperback: 112 pages

Projects to help you build a world of smarter things

1. Learn how to interface various sensors and actuators to the Arduino Yún and send this data in the cloud.

2. Explore the possibilities offered by the Internet of Things by using the Arduino Yún to upload measurements to Google Docs, upload pictures to Dropbox, and send live video streams to YouTube.

3. Learn how to use the Arduino Yún as the brain of a robot that can be completely controlled via Wi-Fi.

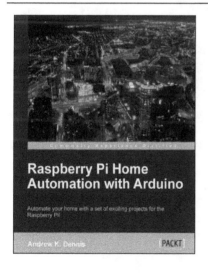

Raspberry Pi Home Automation with Arduino

ISBN: 978-1-84969-586-2   Paperback: 176 pages

Automate your home with a set of exciting projects for the Raspberry Pi!

1. Learn how to dynamically adjust your living environment with detailed step-by-step examples.

2. Discover how you can utilize the combined power of the Raspberry Pi and Arduino for your own projects.

3. Revolutionize the way you interact with your home on a daily basis.

Please check **www.PacktPub.com** for information on our titles

www.ingramcontent.com/pod-product-compliance
Lightning Source LLC
Chambersburg PA
CBHW060157060326
40690CB00018B/4142